Robin,

Happy 60th!

Love.

SMILE OR GET OUT OF THE KITCHEN

AH

ADAM HANDLING

FOREWORD

In 2013, Adam walked into the Masterchef: The Professionals studio to take part.

In his first test – an invention to create any dish, savoury or sweet – I still recall his dessert of sweet potato panna cotta with meringue... it was wonderful.

Adam caught my attention on the set, as well as off, as a skilled and naturally-talented young chef.

He went on to impress Michel Roux Jr. in the next rounds and it is such a joy, for both Michel and I, when you see a rare talent walk into the kitchen.

Throughout the competition Adam was forced to look at himself, his emotional journey through his career and it reconnected his love for Asian flavours – this really came through as his cooking developed.

Adam was one of the strongest contenders who was cooking consistently throughout and it was tough to see him lose out in the final round. But I believe that this hurdle was meant to happen, because when things come too easy in life, we tend to lose focus on reality.

Adam is now cooking stronger than ever, and is heading for the bright lights.

He was, for me always, the one to watch!

Monica Galetti

SMILE OR GET OUT OF THE KITCHEN

First edition printed in 2014 in the UK

ISBN: 978-0-9928981-2-0

Written: Adam Handling, Andy Waple

Edited: Phil Turner, Rachel Heward
James Highmore

Photography: Tim Green

Additional Photography: Lucie Brooks

Design: Paul Cocker

Contributors: Nick Hallam, Sarah Koriba

Published by Meze Publishing
Blind Mice Media Ltd
Unit 1 Beehive Works
Milton Street
Sheffield S3 7WL
www.mezepublishing.co.uk
Tel: 0114 275 7709

CONTENTS

ACKNOWLEDGEMENTS

I'd like to thank the following people who've been a huge support
to me during my daily life and career to date:

Victoria Rankine without who I would never have come some far, you pushed me on to
strive and achieve everything – so a big thank you.

My family, for your constant and unwavering support over the years.

My amazing sous chefs and very good friends, **Steven Kerr** and **Jonathan McNeil**.
I love you both for all your support, you are the only people I truly trust to run my kitchens on
a daily basis. I'm so lucky to have had you both working with me for over half of my career
and pushing me to achieve all we have together.

My team, for supporting me and the restaurant.

Lucie Brooks, for creating and designing my brand.

Michel Roux Jr. and **Monica Galetti** for driving me beyond where I thought was possible
and re-igniting my desire.

Chef Massimo Bottura, for showing me that great food always has meaning and teaching
me to cook with my emotions.

Karen Ross and everyone at **ShineTV** for elevating my profile beyond even my own
expectations. I'd recommend the experience to anyone – even the sleepless nights!

To **Nikki Baker** – my on-screen mom!

Douglas McHugh, the GM at **St. Ermin's Hotel**, for all your belief and support as well as
all the other fantastic people supporting me on my journey.

My publishers, **Phil Turner**, **Paul Cocker** and **Tim Green** from **Meze Publishing** –
here's to many more books.

Aubrey Allen's, for our guided tour and photo opportunities.

Stuart Stevens and **David Mason** from Global Harvest for supporting me in and out of
the kitchen

Lastly, but certainly most importantly – to **my diners** – the people who make it worthwhile

Adam Handling

SMILE OR GET OUT
OF THE KITCHEN

The title of this book sums up my approach to life and work – whatever you do, do it well, but make sure you enjoy it.

That's not to say you can afford to be complacent, far from it. Happiness and satisfaction only come through hard work and pushing yourself beyond your boundaries.

This is really the purpose of my first cookbook, published to coincide with the launch of my restaurant, Adam Handling at Caxton.

As you flick through the pages and witness the beautiful photography and glance at some of the exotic ingredients, you may be mistaken in thinking the recipes are ahead of your expertise. Nothing could be further from the truth. Beyond the visual execution of my dishes lies a simplicity that anyone can grasp.

It is a book for home cooks who, like me, really do give a damn about food. It's for those who want to set off on a journey to learn about the intertwining relationships of the different tastes and the flavours that can be extracted from the fantastic array of ingredients the world has given us. You will discover how some seemingly impossible combinations can really work in surprising harmony and dance on your taste buds. Trying these recipes at home will stretch your imagination to its limits, and above all, it will be fun.

I'd like to think the book could also be of value to fellow professionals. I do not mean this in a condescending way as I am young and still have much to learn. But I believe chefs should strive to inspire each other and feed off the creative juices of their peers. Among my personal inspirations have been some great chefs; Tom Aikens, in my early days in London, the awesome Sat Bains, and most of all by the Italian master, Massimo Bottura, who I met at his restaurant Osteria Francescana when I was filming for Masterchef: The Professionals. My sous chefs and best friends, Steven Kerr and Jonathan McNeil also constantly inspire me.

I don't want people to think my recipes are not to be tampered with. The book is not a bible, even I take inspiration from books – my favourite being 'Too many chiefs only one Indian' by Sat Bains.

I'd encourage readers to substitute ingredients and test to see if they work. I want to encourage self-progression, so feel free to change things. Add things, take them away, make dishes bigger and better, and you will be fine.

PUSHING BEYOND
THE BOUNDARIES

My personal style revolves around big flavours, unusual combinations, immediate taste sensations and a touch of nostalgia. I hate pretention and style-over-substance. My dishes have to be tasty – I want diners to be knocked over by the flavours from their first mouthful of food.

They say people judge a book by its cover and a plate of food by its looks. But if you open the book and find that it's boring you, stop and put it down. It is the same with food. It may look good but it fails if the first taste doesn't hit you in the mouth with that "wow" factor.

I am very inquisitive by nature and I like to push ingredients to the limits of their potential. This comes through my creativity that I developed from my family background, training and travels, but also through a lot of hard work in the kitchen. A potential taste combination might come into my head but it is only through rigorous research, testing, tasting, changing, and tasting again that it will stand a chance of making it on to my menu.

I like Asian influences and they form an important element of everything I do. The Japanese are ingenious with food. Their flavours, techniques, attitudes and philosophy towards dishes are remarkable and their methodical understanding is just phenomenal. They have respect for just about everything and all of this is the reason why Japan has more Michelin stars than any other country, including France.

UNEXPECTED HARMONIES

Michel Roux Jr. used this expression to sum up my food on Masterchef and I was phenomenally honoured by what I considered to be a perfect accolade.

I served him a dish of piglet belly and octopus with smoked mussel consommé and seaweed powder. Before he tasted it he said it was crazy; it would not work because there were too many flavours fighting against each other. He tasted it and said it was just incredible.

This dish is a good example of the way I strive to combine ingredients that perhaps you would not think would work together. You can try it for yourself from the recipe in this book.

Another example is lavender with duck. Traditionally duck is paired with sweet tasting ingredients, such as sauces from cherries or oranges, though we wondered if anybody had tried it with lavender. I thought it might work so we did the research and tried it in the kitchen to discover that a lavender glaze worked very well with the gameness of the meat. It's all about being inquisitive and developing an understanding of the taste profiles of each component, seeing if they work in harmony.

It's about testing the balance of tastes and flavours – play around, practice, fail, practice again... and succeed.

DREAM AS BIG AS YOU WANT BUT KEEP YOUR FEET ON THE GROUND

I was born in Dundee, but being part of a military family it was inevitable that I would never put roots down anywhere. I left Scotland, aged four, travelling widely.

My parents are very health-conscious. Mum spent a lot of time baking and there were always homemade breads, cakes and biscuits on the go.

From being a wee boy I would help her in the kitchen, and my love of cooking and quality ingredients was born.

At 16 I took a job as an apprentice in the kitchens at the famous Gleneagles Hotel. My passion for pastry blossomed in to a thirst for knowledge of all other types of cooking. Today, I remain as inquisitive as ever. As others will tell you, I'm the type of person who hates not knowing everything.

All good chefs need to work in London at some stage of their career so I decided I wanted to use my experience gained from Gleneagles to get in to some top London kitchens. With my parents' support I could afford to work for free and feed off the knowledge of some of the best kitchen brigades.

With that experience under my belt I moved on to become demi-chef de partie at the Malmaison Hotel in Newcastle.

After three years of great fun and hard work I moved back to Scotland becoming junior sous at the Fairmont St Andrews. There I won the Scottish Young Chef of the Year award and became operational head chef of fine dining at age 21.

But this period in my life was a defining moment. I had became frustrated at not gaining a Michelin star and started to hate my job.

My partner suggested I left to travel the world. I had gained fine dining experience but hadn't worked in a kitchen catering for large volumes of diners which led me to apply for a post on the luxury cruise liner Crystal Serenity, which carried 600 passengers.

After a six-month tour I left to travel the world, spending many hours in culinary schools in Japan and South East Asia in particular. I learned their individual fundamentals and the unbelievable detail of authentic culinary styles that had been passed down through generations.

By the time I returned to London I became head chef of the iconic St Ermin's Hotel in Westminster. I was full of enthusiasm and with a thirst to showcase my new-found knowledge.

It was at the St Ermin's Caxton Grill that another defining moment in my life occurred. I had seen the BBC TV programme Masterchef: The Professionals and decided that it was a challenge I would relish. It was the best decision I have taken in my professional career and I can only say that the whole experience was life-changing – not just for my career, but also for the way I looked at food.

It was the most rewarding, yet scary experience, which challenged every emotion. I felt from the beginning that if I messed up, everything I had worked for would be down the drain and I'd have ruined my career. I made a mistake in the final and I was devastated. But Britain seemed to understand that I had been true to myself and the experience has been so good for me. I'd recommend any chef to aspire to get on the programme; just be yourself, don't be arrogant because if you are and you mess up you are ruined.

It was on Masterchef that I was introduced to Massimo Bottura. He is the most inspirational man I have ever met. He was a life-changing genius who pushed me to think about food in a completely different way. He said to me, "Dream as big as you want, but keep your feet on the ground because you still have to achieve it."

ADAM HANDLING AT CAXTON: RUSTIC REFINEMENT AND A TOUCH OF NOSTALGIA

Opening my first restaurant was another chapter in my career. It's a reflection of my values concerning food and the surroundings I like it to be enjoyed in.

Dining out is a social occasion and as our busy lives dictate that we cook less at home the experience needs to be relaxed and informal.

You will not find white table linen in my restaurant and gone are the traditional white porcelain plates – I hate formality and for me the food should be able to sing for itself.

The feel is what I call 'rustically refined' – chunky wooden tables and my own hand-thrown oriental crockery.

Japanese crockery is so beautiful. It makes the food stand out a little more and it shows character. Sourcing was difficult so I decided to create my own brand. All the pieces are hand made, hand painted and each is unique. They are very heavy, but if they get chipped in the kitchen we will still use them – they add to the rustic quirkiness.

To help bring out a relaxed atmosphere, the menu contains little hints of nostalgia with passing references to flavours you may remember from your childhood. I want to put a smile on your face by providing a flashback, perhaps a reminder of something your granny used to make or a taste from a childhood picnic.

I have my own nostalgia in my tasting menus. The salmon dish takes me back to winning the British Culinary Federation Chef of the Year Award, and my lobster in yellow curry reminds me of the little old woman who taught me the cooking skills of her generation in a culinary school in Thailand.

Behind the scenes we teach the front of house staff to work in a relaxed, personable manner yet with an understated awareness of each table's individual requirements. Little touches like that make all the difference.

UMAMI – IT'S ALL A MATTER OF TASTE

There is a great deal of creativity, forward-thinking, research and testing that goes on in our kitchen to produce dishes that stand out with flavours that zing.

This book does all that research and hard work for you, allowing you to concentrate on buying the very best ingredients and then following the recipes.

But one purpose is to inspire you to learn about taste profiles and flavours and how they can combine to make balanced, harmonious dishes.

You will find many Japanese and South East Asian ingredients in the recipes. My travels there were absolutely inspirational, and since then I have always used their uniqueness to produce the taste impacts I am looking for.

For generations it was thought that humans recognised four taste profiles – bitter, sweet, sour and salty. About 100 years ago the Japanese discovered the fifth taste sensation – umami – that is one of the most important tastes for giving impact to my recipes.

Umami is sometimes described as savoury; it derives from naturally occurring monosodium glutamate in a wide range of diverse foods from Parmesan and tomatoes, through to soy sauce and the various mushrooms and seaweeds so precious to the Japanese. I use Japanese ingredients that are umami dominant in just about everything I cook. They give a certain rich mouthfeel to the food that cannot be replicated.

Each recipe in this book has a scale out of ten, that explains the balance of the five taste profiles. There is always a dominant taste sensation, but others are used as well for balance, harmony and contrast. I hope these charts will give you a better understanding of the thought processes used to make up the recipes.

The nibbles on my tasting menu provide an illustration of what I mean. Each small dish is designed to introduce the diner to the five sensations. They intertwine to make the mouth feel alive. Each dish has a different dominant taste profile so the whole course is a voyage of discovery. For example, the Parmesan madeleines have a headline sweetness, contrasted with umami, the pickled cauliflower is predominately umami, while the crisp pig's head has a salty headline from the anchovies. The sour highlight of the beetroot wakes up your mouth before you taste contrasting umami and sweetness.

GIVE A DAMN ABOUT YOUR FOOD AND ENJOY!

I hope you enjoy this book. Above all be inquisitive and think ahead to discover new flavour combinations.

We've also included a handy glossary and basics section at the back of the book that explains some of the 'cheffy' terms and ingredients in more detail.

Most important of all, interpret my style, research and come up with your own idea, then try it, taste it, try it again and change the dish for the better, and if it works – feel good about it!

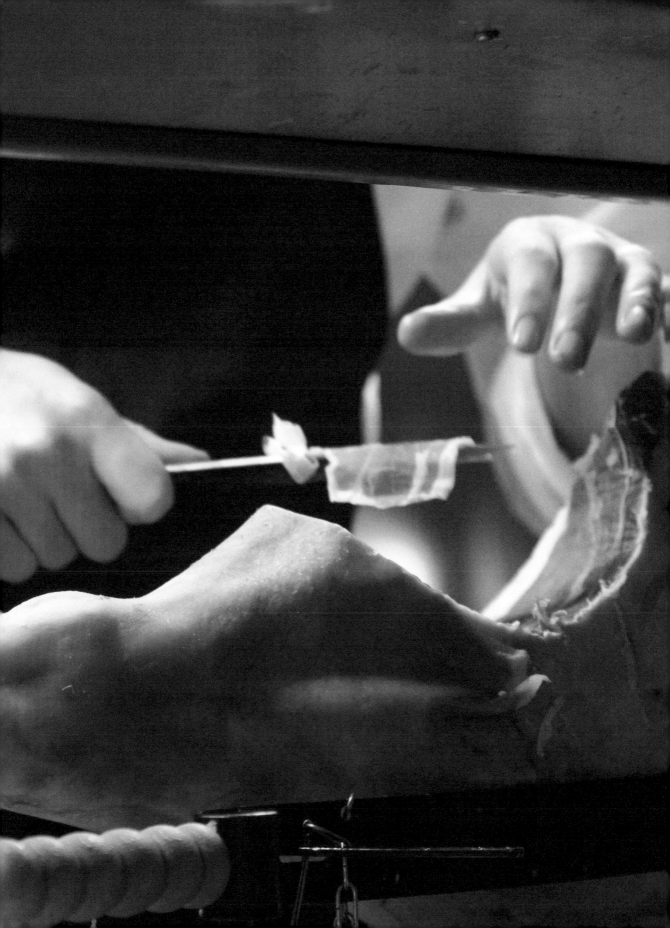

STARTERS

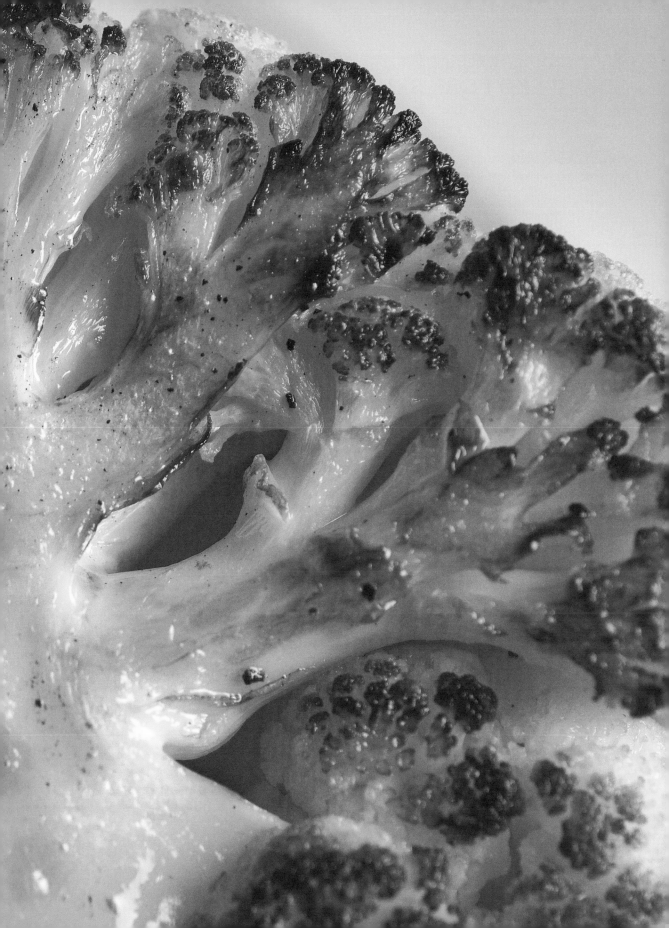

DEVILLED PORK SKINS WITH YUZU MAYO

TASTE PROFILE:

These prawn cracker style pork skins are light and bubbly with a predominantly sweet chilli seven spice seasoning from Japan. The yuzu dressing is sweet, bitter and sour all in one; creating some really big flavours.

Serves: 8-10

Sweet:	0 1 2 3 4
Sour:	0 1 2 3 4 5 6
Bitter:	0 1 2 3
Salty:	0 1 2 3 4 5 6 7 8
Umami:	0 1 2 3 4 5 6 7 8

FOR THE YUZU MAYONNAISE

2 large egg yolks

1 tsp Dijon mustard

Salt and pepper to season

275ml pomace oil

2 tsp white wine vinegar

60g yuzu juice

Add egg, mustard and seasoning to a small food processor and blitz

While blending slowly trickle in oil until the mixture is thick and creamy

Add white wine vinegar and yuzu juice

FOR THE PORK CRACKLING

2 whole belly pork skins

1 tsp togarashi seasoning

Vegetable oil for frying

Place the belly pork skins in boiling water and cook for 1 hour 30 minutes

Drain, cool and scrape off all the excess fat

Dry in the oven for a few hours at 100°C

Deep fry at 180°C

Sprinkle with togarashi seasoning

PICKLED CAULIFLOWER WITH BURNT MUSHROOM BUTTER

TASTE PROFILE:

For a vegetarian dish, this is absolutely packed with flavour – containing really high taste profile notes across the board.

Serves: 10-15

Sweet: ⓪①②③④⑤
Sour: ⓪①②③④⑤
Bitter: ⓪
Salty: ⓪
Umami: ⓪①②③④⑤⑥⑦⑧

FOR THE AMAZU PICKLING LIQUID

200ml rice wine vinegar

150g sugar

12g salt

Bring all to the boil until the salt and sugar has dissolved

FOR THE CAULIFLOWER

1 baby cauliflower

Cut the cauliflower into baby florets

Ensure the stalks are left long

Warm the pickling liquid and pour it over the cauliflower in a bowl

Cover with cling film and leave to sit for 2 hours

FOR THE MUSHROOM PURÉE

200g shitake mushrooms

3 banana shallots

4 cloves garlic

Vegetable oil for frying

20ml soy sauce

Thinly slice the mushrooms, shallots and garlic

In a pan add a splash of vegetable oil

Add the shallots and garlic and cook slowly until caramelised

Add the mushrooms and cook slowly until pan is dry

Add the soy sauce and then blend it all in a mixer

Pass through a fine sieve into a bowl to remove all lumps and serve

FOR THE BURNT MUSHROOM BUTTER

100g beurre noisette (see basics)

150ml dark chicken stock (see basics)

10g balsamic vinegar

50g mushroom purée

Salt

Warm the beurre noisette and add the mushroom purée

Blend together

Add chicken stock and balsamic vinegar

Taste and season with salt

Place in a bowl and rest bowl in ice water

Whisk to a fluffy consistency as it cools

FOR THE GARNISH

Mushroom and seaweed powder

Micro chard

BEETROOT, BEETROOT AND MORE BEETROOT

TASTE PROFILE:

With a huge bang of unexpected flavour – this is a dish to make you smile. It has the earthiness of the panna cotta offset by the sharpness of the yuzu gel, creating a truly unanticipated but enchanting harmony.

Serves: 8-10

Sweet: ⓿①②③④❺❻
Sour: ⓿①②③④❺❻
Bitter: ⓿①②③④
Salty: ⓿
Umami: ⓿①②③④❺❻❼

FOR THE SUGAR TUBES

140g sugar

30g water

100g glucose

Mix and gently boil the ingredients to make a light caramel

Pour onto a silicone mat or greaseproof tray

Allow to cool

Break up from mat and blitz to a fine powder in a mixer

Using a rectangular stencil or cookie cutter sprinkle the mixture generously on to a silicone mat, or greaseproof tray

Bake in the oven at 180°C for 3 minutes then allow the sugar to cool slightly before removing

Carefully wrap the sugar around a cylinder or thick wooden spoon to form a tube then place aside to set

FOR THE BEETROOT PICKLE

1 raw beetroot, peeled and finely diced

200ml Amazu pickling liquid (see basics)

Cut the beetroot into small dice

Warm the Amazu and pour over beetroot

Cover with cling film leave for 2 hours

FOR THE BEETROOT PANNA COTTA

1½ sheets gelatine

125g beetroot juice

75g double cream

Pinch of salt

Soak gelatine in cold water

Bring juice and cream up to the boil

Remove from heat and add soaked gelatine

Add seasoning

Pour into a container and allow to set in the fridge for approximately 1½ hours

FOR THE BEETROOT AND YUZU GEL

200g yuzu

150ml beetroot juice

125ml stock syrup (see basics)

7g agar

25g sugar

Bring to boil yuzu, beetroot juice and stock syrup

Mix agar and sugar together

When liquid is boiling, whisk in powder

Cook for 30 seconds

Pour into container

Rest in fridge for 2 hours

Blend in mixer until mayonnaise consistency is formed

TO MAKE DISH

Beetroot powder

Ruby chard

100g beetroot, diced

Pipe the panna cotta into the centre of the sugar tubes

Add diced beetroot into tube

Add gel into tube

Finish with panna cotta the other side, ensure panna cotta is on both ends of the tube

Decorate plate with diced pickle

Cover in beetroot powder

Finish with ruby chard

CRAB DOUGHNUTS

TASTE PROFILE:

I've always loved crab with brioche; mixing it with doughnuts makes it even more fun and tastes even better. Freshly cooked doughnuts have a nostalgia to them – reminding me of being a kid at a fairground – and that's what I wanted to bring to this dish.

Serves: 8-10

Sweet: ⓪❶②❸❹
Sour: ⓪
Bitter: ⓪
Salty: ⓪
Umami: ⓪❶②❸❹

FOR THE CRAB

2 large, freshly cooked crabs (approx. 250g crabmeat)

200ml mayonnaise

½ lemon, juiced

Salt and pepper to season

Twist off the claws and legs and separate the body from the main shell

Remove inedible dead man's fingers from the body

Loosen the brown meat in the main shell and spoon in to a bowl

Crack the large claws open and take out the white meat

Prise out the rest of the white meat

Check for shell fragments whilst shredding the crabmeat

Add the mayonnaise

Add lemon and season to taste

FOR THE MAYONNAISE

1 large egg yolk

½ tsp Dijon mustard

Salt and pepper to season

130ml pomace oil

1 tsp white wine vinegar

Add egg, mustard and seasoning to a small food processor and blitz

While blending, slowly trickle in oil

The mixture should be thick and creamy

Add white wine vinegar and season to taste

FOR THE DOUGHNUTS

75g milk

7g fresh yeast

250g T55 bread flour

2g salt

60g sugar

1 large egg (or 2 medium)

33g clarified butter

Oil for deep frying

Warm milk

Add yeast

Leave somewhere warm for 1 hour

Add flour, salt, sugar, egg to a mixer with dough hook attachment

Slowly add milk and stir

Slowly add butter and mix until dough comes away from bowl

Prove for 1 hour

Knock back and roll out into little balls

Deep fry until golden brown

TO ASSEMBLE

Zest of a lemon

Micro herbs

Split the doughnuts in half

Fill with the crab mixture and decorate with lemon zest and micro herbs

PARMESAN MADELEINES, CHICKEN BUTTER

TASTE PROFILE:

Freshly made, hot, cheesy madeleines are fantastic to eat; but serving them with roasted chicken butter takes them to a new level. We all know that the skin is the best part of a roast chicken – which is why we use it in our butter.

Sweet:	⓪①❷③④
Sour:	⓪
Bitter:	⓪①②❸④
Salty:	⓪①②❸④
Umami:	⓪①②③④⑤⑥⑦❽

FOR THE MADELEINES

4 large eggs

225g sugar

195g plain flour

7g salt

3g baking powder

95g Parmesan

50g olive oil

Mix together the egg and sugar until light and fluffy

Fold in flour, salt, baking powder and Parmesan

Add oil

Beat until smooth

Place in piping bag and rest in fridge for an hour

Oil madeleine moulds and pipe in a quarter full

Cook in oven at 175°C for 6-8 minutes

FOR THE CHICKEN BUTTER

120g soft butter

5g seaweed salt

100g dried crisp chicken skins, scraped

Blend all together

Store at room temperature

SWEET AND SOUR SALT AND PEPPER SQUID

Serves: 8

TASTE PROFILE:

Your standard salt and pepper squid is a thing of the past; adding crunchy, crispy herbs and a touch of chilli is what sets this dish apart.

Sweet:	0 1 2 3 4 5 6
Sour:	0 1 2 3 4 5 6
Bitter:	0 1 2
Salty:	0 1 2 3 4 5 6
Umami:	0 1 2 3 4 5 6

FOR THE SWEET AND SOUR PONZU MARINADE

100g rice vinegar

10g soy sauce

5 lemons, juiced

70g sugar

5g sea salt

¾ inch square piece konbu

Stir together all ingredients in a small bowl

Let stand overnight then strain

FOR THE SQUID

500g baby squid

Flour for dusting

Vegetable oil for frying

Salt and pepper to season

Clean the squid by removing the skin and the sack inside the tube, or ask your fishmonger to prepare

Wash properly to make sure there is no grit

With the tentacles, remove the beak, which is the little black circle in the middle under the tentacles, by gently squeezing

Cut the squid in rough uneven pieces

Pour ¾ of the marinade over and let stand for 10 minutes

Shake off marinade

Dust in flour and deep fry

Season with salt and fresh pepper and pour the rest of the marinade over

TO SERVE

Bunch of coriander

1 red chilli, sliced

Oil for frying

Chop the herbs and chilli then fry in hot oil for 5 seconds until crispy

VEGETABLES

GRILLED ASPARAGUS, ORANGE, WOOD SORREL, SLOW COOKED QUAIL EGG

TASTE PROFILE:
My take on boiled eggs and soldiers; I use roasted asparagus finished with a touch of orange and a slow-cooked egg to make a perfect summer salad.

Serves: 5

Sweet:　❶❷❸❹❺
Sour:　❶❷
Bitter:　❶
Salty:　❶❷❸❹
Umami:　❶

FOR THE GRILLED ASPARAGUS

10 green tenderstem asparagus

10 white tenderstem asparagus

10 purple tenderstem asparagus

Remove stalk by snapping asparagus at its natural point

Trim to ensure all are the same size

Divide the asparagus into halves

For the first half, blanch in boiling water, refresh in ice-cold water, pat dry and store in a lined container

To serve grill until charred

Slice the remainder lengthways, thinly and gently, on a mandoline then blanch and refresh immediately, pat dry and store in a lined container

FOR THE CONFIT ORANGE

1 large orange, peel only

Sugar for dusting

100ml stock syrup (see basics)

Peel orange removing all pith

Julienne the orange peel

Dust in sugar

Leave for an hour

Refresh 3 times in the syrup

Leave to cool in the syrup for 24 hours

FOR THE ORANGE DRESSING

½ syrup from confit orange

1 tsp wholegrain mustard

½ tsp chopped baby capers

Picked thyme leaves

2 drops of orange oil

1 lemon, zest only

Combine all

FOR THE LEMON DRESSING

1 egg white

1 lemon

35ml stock syrup (see basics)

Blitz using hand blender

FOR THE SLOW COOKED QUAIL EGG

5 organic quail eggs

Bring a saucepan of water to boil, then turn off the heat

Keeping the shell on, add the eggs directly from the fridge and leave for 35 minutes, this will create a lovely custard texture to the yolks

Gently peel off the shell and serve immediately

TO ASSEMBLE

Handful of wood sorrel

Scatter the asparagus, sorrel and confit orange around the plate

Halve the eggs and add to the plate

Add a spoonful of lemon dressing

Drizzle on the orange dressing and serve

GNOCCHI OF BURNT LEEKS AND PARMA HAM

Serves: 5

TASTE PROFILE:

Not a traditional gnocchi dish. I prefer to pan-roast the gnocchi rather than boil them. They taste like little roast dumplings. Charring the leeks caramelises the natural sugars creating both sweet and bitter tones, which are finished with salty ham.

Sweet: ⓿❶❷❸
Sour: ⓿
Bitter: ⓿❶❷❸❹❺
Salty: ⓿❶❷❸❹
Umami: ⓿❶❷❸❹❺❻❼

FOR THE GNOCCHI

1.2kg red skin potatoes

200g strong flour

2 large eggs

75g Parmesan

Salt, enough to form a layer on a baking tray

Olive oil for frying

Butter

Roast potatoes in a roasting tray layered with salt for at 35 minutes at 180°C

Pass potatoes through a sieve

Make a well with the mashed potatoes

Add the flour, eggs and Parmesan

Season with salt

Roll into cylinders around 2cm in diameter

Cut 3cm pieces from the cylinder and using the back of a fork roll to make gnocchi shapes

Add a little olive oil to a pan and roast off gnocchi until crisp. When golden brown, add a knob of butter and foam up

FOR THE BURNT LEEK

1 leek

Remove the outer layer from the leek and cut into 1 inch pieces

In a hot pan cook the leek on both sides until slightly burnt

Remove from the heat and let them finish cooking

Pop the layers out and keep aside to be put through the sauce

FOR THE SAUCE

200g butter

40g crushed hazelnuts

2 lemons, juiced

100g crème fraîche

Parma ham

Melt butter in a large pan, agitate to create a foam

When golden brown, but not burnt, add the hazelnuts and toast

Add the lemon juice

After the sugars in the lemon juice have cooked out, add the crème fraîche and season

Toss the pan-fried gnocchi into the sauce

Finish with Parma ham and burnt leek

CAULIFLOWER AND CHEESE TAGLIATELLE

TASTE PROFILE:

Cauliflower is one of my favourite vegetables and having different contrasts, from burnt purée to lightly blanched florets and raw pieces makes this a cauliflower lover's dream. Every time I've entered this dish into a competition, I've won!

Serves: 6

Sweet: ⓪❶❷❸
Sour: ⓪❶❷❸
Bitter: ⓪
Salty: ⓪
Umami: ⓪❶❷❸❹❺❻❼

FOR THE PASTA DOUGH

1kg '00' flour
8 egg yolks
8 whole eggs
10ml olive oil
10ml water, warm
Pinch of saffron
Fine ground salt and pepper

Place the flour on a board and make a well in the centre
Add all eggs and olive oil into the centre of the well
Warm the water, add the saffron and seasoning together and add into the well in the centre of the flour
With a fork gently mix in the flour little by little until a dough-like consistency is reached, adding a little more water if necessary
Knead until smooth then cling film and rest in fridge

MAKING THE TAGLIATELLE

Semolina flour, for dusting
Olive oil

Roll out the pasta to around 2cm thick until see through
Using a knife cut strips and dust in semolina flour to dry out slightly
Blanch in salted water with a splash of olive oil in when needed

FOR THE CAULIFLOWER PURÉE

1 large 500g cauliflower, or use cauliflower scraps
65g butter
50ml dark chicken stock (see basics)
Salt
Splash single cream
½ lemon, juiced

Cut the cauliflower in to 1 inch thick pieces
Melt butter in frying pan
Fry cauliflower, mixing so butter is frothed
Cook until cauliflower is golden brown. Don't worry if it burns, this adds to the flavour
Add chicken stock
Add splash of cream
Pass through a sieve and then blitz
Season and add a squeeze of lemon

FOR THE CHEESE SAUCE

250g single cream
175g Parmesan cheese
100g whole milk
45g Dijon mustard

Boil the single cream
Grate the Parmesan and add to the blender
Pour over the hot cream and blend on high for 2 minutes
Pass through a sieve and add the milk and Dijon mustard
Mix the cauliflower purée and cheese sauce together in a ratio of 60% cheese sauce to 40% cauliflower purée
Toss the pasta in the sauce

GARNISH

2 small cauliflowers, in different colours if possible
Salt and pepper to season
1 lemon, juiced

Cut into small florets and blanch in boiling salted water for 2 minutes
Mix into the pasta adding a touch of lemon juice
Season with salt and pepper

COURGETTE FLOWERS, GOAT'S CURD, HONEY

TASTE PROFILE:

Courgette flowers are only available for one month of the year (around June-July) and are always on my menu when in season. Stuffing them with goat's cheese and dipping in a light tempura creates a fanatsic texture – I can eat a bowlful! I use my own honey but any good quality honey works fine.

Serves: 5

Sweet: ⓿❶❷❸❹❺❻❼
Sour: ⓿❶❷
Bitter: ⓿❶❷
Salty: ⓿❶❷❸❹❺❻
Umami: ⓿❶❷❸❹❺❻

FOR THE ROAST SHALLOTS

5 banana shallots

50ml olive oil

4 sprigs thyme

Salt and pepper to season

Finely dice the shallots

In heavy-based pan, add olive oil, shallots and thyme

Cook until golden

Season and allow to cool

FOR THE GOAT'S CHEESE

200g soft goat's cheese

50g thick crème fraîche

2 tbsp roast shallot mixture

Salt and pepper to season

When the roast shallots are cold combine with the goat's cheese and crème fraîche then beat until smooth

Season to taste

FOR THE TEMPURA BATTER

100g cornflour

100g plain flour

30g sesame seeds

200ml sparkling water

Salt and pepper to season

Add the dry ingredients to a bowl

Pour in the sparkling water gradually

Fold together and season to taste

Store in fridge

FOR THE COURGETTES

10 courgettes

Slice the courgettes in half, keeping the flower intact, if small leave courgettes whole

Roll balls of the goat's cheese and freeze for 5 minutes

When chilled place the goat's cheese inside the courgette flowers

Dip into tempura batter

Fry until golden crisp

HONEY AND THYME DRESSING

100g St Ermin's honey

40g thyme leaves, picked

15g olive oil

Each thyme leaf must be picked individually, no stalks

Combine all the ingredients and whisk to make a dressing

MACARONI CHEESE, GARLIC, PEAS, MUSHROOMS

TASTE PROFILE:
Who doesn't like the homely flavours of mac & cheese?
I love playing with comfort-food dishes and just simply
plating them up in an innovative way.

Serves: 8

Sweet: ❶❶❷❸
Sour: ❶❶❷❸
Bitter: ❶❶❷❸❹
Salty: ❶❶❷❸❹
Umami: ❶❶❷❸❹❺❻❼❽❾

FOR THE MACARONI

1 pack 30cm macaroni tubes

In a saucepan of boiling water, blanch the pasta until it's
al dente and refresh in cold water

FOR THE TRUFFLE MORNAY

50g butter

50g plain flour, sieved

120g whole milk

300g double cream

150g Gruyère

200g Parmesan

80g Dijon mustard

1 small truffle

6 egg yolks

Salt

In a heavy-based saucepan, melt the butter, sieve in the
flour and cook to form a paste

Cook for 3 minutes, until you have a white roux, known
as a roux blanc

Next in a separate saucepan gently warm the milk and
cream

Add the cheeses to the roux blanc and cook out until
spilt and dissolved

Bring back the roux mixture by adding in the warmed
milk and cream, one ladle at a time until the béchamel
is made when you have achieved a smooth, silky
consistency

Remove from the heat and add the mustard then season
to taste

Pass through a fine sieve then add a grating of truffle
and the egg yolks

Store in a container, topped with a cartouche

TO ASSEMBLE THE MACARONI

Spray silver metal ring with oil to prevent sticking

Cut the pasta just longer than the rings

Stand them end-up in the ring working all around until it
is fully packed

Pipe the béchamel into the holes and the gaps of the
pasta and allow to cool

Cut off the excess pasta at the top to make a neat finish

Store in the fridge until needed

To serve, place in a oven at 180°C for 8-10 minutes then
remove the ring

FOR THE MUSHROOM AND PEA FRICASSÉE

1 shallot, finely diced

2 cloves garlic, minced

1 punnet wild mushrooms

Knob of butter

Shelled fresh peas

Shelled fresh broad beans

Small handful red veined sorrel

Salt and pepper to season

In a hot pan, cook the finely diced shallot and garlic

Add the mushrooms, then add the butter and allow to
foam

Add the peas, broad beans and sorrel and warm through
for a further minute

Season to taste

TO SERVE

Pea shoots

Fresh truffle

Place the macaroni in the oven at 180°C to warm
through

Serve the fricassée in a side dish

Garnish the macaroni with pea shoots and fresh truffle

PEACH, RADISH, DANDELION SALAD
WITH WASABI PURÉE

TASTE PROFILE:

A sweet and bitter dish, the little kick of wasabi really enhances the natural sugars of the peach and makes a nice, light salad.

Serves: 5

Sweet: ⓿❶❷❸❹❺❻
Sour: ⓿❶❷❸❹
Bitter: ⓿❶❷❸❹❺❻❼❽❾
Salty: ⓿❶❷
Umami: ⓿❶❷❸❹❺

FOR THE PEACHES

3 ripe peaches

Cracked black pepper

Olive oil

Cut all the peaches into segments

Drizzle them with olive oil and cracked black pepper

Using one of the peaches, lightly blowtorch, or place under the grill, until caremlised in its own sugars and so slighlty bitter

FOR THE DANDELIONS

1 bunch dandelions leaves

Buy the dandelion leaves from a good greengrocer or farmshop

Prepare the dandelion leaves by washing and removing the root

Set aside

FOR THE DRESSING

80g grapeseed oil

60g soy sauce

80g rice wine vinegar

12g sugar

5g black pepper

15g wholegrain mustard

1 shallot, finely diced

Combine all the ingredients and whisk briefly

FOR THE GARNISH

Long radishes, thinly sliced

Toasted pistachios

Wasabi purée (see basics)

Toss the dandelion leaves, sliced radish and toasted pistachios in the dressing and place on the plate

Add dots of wasabi purée to the plate

Scatter the peaches amongst the salad leaves

CELERIAC VELOUTÉ

TASTE PROFILE:

A really intense, earthy soup; this is also perfect as a base for a fuller dish. Ham hock works especially well.

Sweet:	⓿❶❷❸❹
Sour:	⓿
Bitter:	⓿❶❷
Salty:	⓿❶❷
Umami:	⓿❶❷❸❹❺❻

FOR THE VELOUTÉ

1 celeriac

5 shallots

3 cloves garlic

Olive oil

200g butter

Bunch thyme, chopped

800ml cream

400ml milk

Salt and white pepper

1 lemon, juice

50g sugar

Splash of milk, to finish

Knob of butter, to finish

Peel and dice celeriac

Dice the shallots and garlic

Put the diced celeriac, shallots and garlic on a tray, drizzle with olive oil

Place in an oven and cook until golden brown on 180°C

Once the vegetables have roasted, melt butter in a heavy-based saucepan

Add the roasted vegetables and chopped thyme and soften in the butter

Add cream and milk

Season with salt and pepper to taste

Place a cartouche over the velouté, lower the heat and gently cook until celeriac is tender

Once cooked, blitz until smooth

Pass through a sieve, season then add sugar and lemon juice

Just before serving, add a splash of cold milk and knob of cold butter and use a hand blender to aerate the soup

FOR THE CHEDDAR CHEESE WAFER

100g puff pasty

50g good cheddar cheese, grated

1 egg yolk

Micro-herbs

1 tbsp crème fraîche

Preheat the oven to 180°C

Thinly roll out the puff pastry

Cut into 2cm x 15cm strips

Brush with egg yolk and sprinkle with grated cheese

Place on a greaseproof tray and bake for 8-9 minutes until golden brown

Garnish with crème fraîche and micro-herbs

SALT BAKED CELERIAC, TRUFFLE, APPLES, DATES, CREAM CHEESE

Serves: 5

TASTE PROFILE:

Salt roasting root vegetables removes the moisture but intensifies the natural flavours. The serving of sweet dates, salty celeriac and acidic cream cheese is a perfectly balanced combination.

Sweet:	0 1 2
Sour:	0 1 2 3 4 5 6
Bitter:	0 1 2 3 4
Salty:	0 1 2 3 4 5 6 7 8
Umami:	0 1 2 3 4 5 6 7 8

FOR THE SALT BAKED CELERIAC

1 small celeriac
350g fine table salt
Olive oil

Scrub celeriac, removing all grit and dirt
Roll in fine table salt
Bake at 210°C for 45 minutes until tender but not mushy
Allow to cool naturally then remove the salt crust
Thinly slice and drizzle with olive oil

FOR THE CREAM CHEESE

200g good quality cream cheese
Truffle oil
Pinch of sugar

Whip the cream cheese with a touch of truffle oil
Season to taste with a pinch of sugar

FOR THE ROAST DATES

100g dates
100g butter

Dice dates
Roast in butter until golden brown

FOR THE GARNISH

1 Granny Smith apple, julienne
Chervil
Fresh truffle for grating
Seaweed salt
Celeriac crumb (see basics)

HERITAGE CARROT SALAD, TARRAGON AND LEMON

TASTE PROFILE:

A lovely little autumn starter with the contrast of pickled carrots, yoghurt dressing and thinly sliced raw carrots. The little kick from the togarashi seasoning makes a vibrant, colourful dish.

Sweet: ⓪①❷❸④
Sour: ⓪①❷❸❹❺❻
Bitter: ⓪
Salty: ⓪
Umami: ⓪

FOR THE PICKLED CARROTS

1 bunch baby rainbow carrots
2 large carrots

Small dice the large carrots
Thinly slice baby carrots

FOR THE PICKLING LIQUID

75ml carrot juice
75ml Amazu
5 coriander seeds
50ml olive oil

Mix together
Warm slightly
Pour over the two types of carrots, in separate bowls
Cover and place in fridge for minimum 1 hour

FOR THE DRESSING

45ml lemon juice
20g honey
12g sugar
90g natural yoghurt
Small handful coriander and chervil
Salt and pepper to season

Bring lemon juice to boil with honey and sugar
Pour over the yoghurt
Add herbs and blend
Season with salt and pepper

FOR THE GARNISH

Carrot tops
Hazelnuts
Burnt lemon juice (see basics)
Togarashi seasoning

ROAST CAULIFLOWER, CURRY, COCONUT, SULTANAS

TASTE PROFILE:

Butter-poached cauliflower steaks, lightly spiced then served with sweet sultanas – the classic components of an Indian curry – presented with a modern twist and with no sauce.

Serves: 6

Sweet: ⓪❶❷❸❹
Sour: ⓪
Bitter: ⓪
Salty: ⓪❶❷
Umami: ⓪❶❷❸❹

FOR THE ROASTED CAULIFLOWER

1 extra-large cauliflower
Curry oil (see basics)
Salt and pepper to season
Butter for poaching

Slice thickly through the florets
Add cauliflower to a baking tray
Poach in the butter until tender at 120°C for 40 minutes
Remove from heat
Allow to cool
When ready to use toast in a pan until golden brown
Season both sides with salt and pepper

FOR THE CURRIED SULTANAS

100g sultanas, soaked in water
50ml seasoned curry oil

Soak sultanas in water to plump
Pan-fry in hot curry oil, be careful as they will spit

FOR THE PICKLED CAULIFLOWER

1 cauliflower
100g light brown sugar
200g white balsamic
50ml white wine vinegar
10g salt
15g mustard seeds

Cut cauliflower into small florets
Make a pickling liquid with the sugar, white balsamic, white wine vinegar, salt and mustard seeds then bring to a boil
Place the florets in bowl and pour over the pickling liquid
Cover and leave for a minimum of 2 hours

FOR THE CAULIFLOWER PURÉE

500g cauliflower scraps
65g butter
50ml dark chicken stock (see basics)
Salt for seasoning
Splash of cream
½ lemon, juice

Dice the cauliflower in to 1 inch thick pieces
Melt butter in frying pan
Fry cauliflower, mixing so butter is frothed
Cook until cauliflower is golden brown. Don't worry if it overburns, this adds to the flavour
Add chicken stock
Add splash of cream
Pass through a sieve and blitz
Season and add a squeeze of lemon

FOR THE CURRY PURÉE

4 large white Italian onions
5 cloves garlic
280g butter
5 apples, sliced
10g thyme leaves
40g good masala powder
100ml chicken stock
1 stick lemongrass, crushed
Salt and pepper to season
½ lemon, juice

Thinly slice the onions and garlic
Melt the butter in a large saucepan
Add the sliced apples and cook for 50 minutes until soft and tender
Sprinkle in the thyme and curry powder and cook out for a couple of minutes
Add the chicken stock and lemongrass then cook until reduced
Remove the lemongrass, season to taste and blitz until smooth then pass through a sieve
Finish with the juice of the half a lemon

FOR THE GARNISH

Grated coconut flesh
Whole toasted almond snippets
Green apple
Chervil
Ponzu dressing

DUCK EGG, DRY SALAD AND GOAT'S CURD

TASTE PROFILE:

Salads can be boring. So to create something exciting, pick your leaves and dry them out in the oven and use as a crispy salad. The slow cooked duck eggs combined with the soft goat's cheese and the textured leaves is a joy in the mouth.

Serves: 6

Sweet:	0
Sour:	0
Bitter:	0 1 2 3 4 5 6
Salty:	0 1 2 3 4 5
Umami:	0 1 2 3 4 5 6 7 8 9

FOR THE DUCK EGGS

6 large organic duck eggs

Place eggs in a saucepan of water

Bring the water to 63°C

Cook slowly for 25 minutes

Place in ice-cold water to chill down

When serving, place in warm water to remove the chill, then crack and shell

FOR THE GOAT'S CURD MOUSSE

500g goat's curd

500g goat's cheese

Splash truffle oil

Salt and pepper to season

Peel the goat's cheese

Beat the curd with the cheese and truffle oil

Season to taste

Place in container and leave at room temperature until ready to serve

FOR THE BURNT LEMON

2 lemons

40ml stock syrup (see basics)

Cut lemons in half

Burn the cut surface on a stove top or flat-bottomed pan

When burnt, squeeze the juice into the stock syrup

Bring to boil

Use as a dressing

FOR THE DILL OIL

1 bunch dill

20ml water

30ml vegetable oil

Pick the dill and blanch in salted water for 7 seconds

Refresh in iced water

Lay out on a tray and leave to dry slightly

Add to blender and add vegetable oil

Blend for 1 minute then place blender jug in fridge for 10 minutes

Repeat process 2 more times

Once finally blended cool instantly to preserve colour

FOR THE DRY SALAD

Rocket leaves

Thinly sliced fennel

Radicchio

Baby gem lettuce

Lay thinly on a tray and dry in the oven at 100°C for 3 hours

When dry remove carefully

PEAS, PICKLED GIROLLES, WASABI AND BLOSSOMS

TASTE PROFILE:

Fresh peas are quite simply one of my favourite things to eat so I created a dish for National Chef of the Year that was my homage to them. This works so well because the dish is counter-balanced with Parmesan custard and fresh, vibrant dill.

Serves: 5

Sweet:	⓪①②❸❹❺
Sour:	⓪①②❸❹❺❻
Bitter:	⓪①②❸❹❺
Salty:	⓪
Umami:	⓪❶❷

FOR THE PEA PANNA COTTA

2½ gelatine leaves
200g peas
250ml water
50ml cream
Salt and pepper to season

Soak the gelatine in iced water
Blend the peas with the water until smooth
Bring the cream to the boil and dissolve the gelatine
Add to the pea liquid
Season with salt and pepper when warm
Place in fridge to set for about 1 hour

FOR THE PARMESAN CUSTARD

100ml whole milk
250ml single cream
175g 30 month matured Parmesan
30g truffle, finely chopped

In a saucepan combine the milk and single cream then bring to a boil
Grate Parmesan into a bowl then add to a blender
Pour over the hot cream and blend on high for 2 minutes
Chill in the fridge for 2 hours
Finally chop the truffle into a powder and place on the custard

FOR THE PEAS

50g shelled peas
50ml dill oil (see basics)
Salt and pepper to season

Boil fresh peas for 30 seconds and then refresh in ice-cold water
Shell the peas
Add to dill oil and season to taste

FOR THE SWEET & SOUR WASABI PURÉE

200g good quality wasabi powder
150g sugar
200g palm sugar
150ml Champagne vinegar
500ml bottled water
11g agar

Combine the wasabi powder, sugar, palm sugar, vinegar and water in a saucepan and bring to a boil
When boiling whisk in the agar and cook out for 1 minute
Pass through a fine sieve and leave to set in the fridge for 4 hours
Add to a blender and blend until smooth before serving

FOR THE PICKLED GIROLLES

15 girolles
Amazu pickling liquid (see basics)

Clean and trim the girolles
Boil the pickling the liquid then pour over the trimmed mushrooms
Cover with cling film and leave for 30 minutes

FOR THE GARNISH

Pea blossoms
Micro cucumbers

MAPLE BURNT ONION, HEN'S EGG, PONZU, WILD GARLIC

TASTE PROFILE:

Slow-roasted onions go very sweet, more so with the addition of a good quality maple syrup. The contrast with the sharp ponzu brings it back to the savoury side giving a really good balance of intense flavour.

Serves: 6

Sweet: 0 1 2 3 4
Sour: 0 1 2 3 4 5 6 7 8
Bitter: 0 1 2 3 4 5 6
Salty: 0 1 2 3 4
Umami: 0 1 2 3 4 5 6 7 8 9

FOR THE MAPLE ONION

3 medium onions
150ml rice wine vinegar
100ml maple syrup
50ml muscavado sugar
60g butter
Salt and fresh black pepper

Peel and cut the onions in half
Blacken the onions on the cut side in a hot pan
Place on a baking tray
Mix all the other ingredients together
Pour over onions
Cover the tray with foil
Bake in the oven at 160°C for 45 minutes

FOR THE PONZU

160g rice wine vinegar
85g soy sauce
25g lemon juice

Mix all together and use as a dressing

FOR THE SLOW COOKED HEN'S EGG

6 large organic hen eggs

Bring a saucepan of water to boil, then turn off the heat
Keeping the shell on, add the eggs directly from the fridge and leave for 35 minutes, this will create a lovely custard texture to the yolks
Gently peel off the shell and serve immediately

FOR THE SHALLOT PURÉE

5 shallots
50g butter
20ml olive oil
100ml chicken stock
50ml mirin
Salt and pepper to season

Thinly slice shallots
Add olive oil and butter to a saucepan on high heat
Sweat the shallots until soft and translucent
When moisture has evaporated reduce heat to low
Cook for 30 minutes until shallots are golden and caramelised
Add chicken stock and scrape off the bottom of the pan
Add the mirin
Reduce slightly
Blend until smooth
Season to taste with salt and pepper

FOR THE WILD GARLIC

Handful of wild garlic
Knob of butter
Salt and pepper to season

Wash wild garlic leaves
Cook in a saucepan with a little water and butter for about 45 seconds
Remove and season with salt and pepper

FOR THE GARNISH

Crispy onions
Onion blossom

FISH

HAKE, LEEKS, WASABI, SPRING ONION

FOR THE HAKE

1 whole hake

2 leeks

Remove the fish sides from the bone, taking extra care as hake is extremely delicate

Remove the skin and make sure no bones are left in

Wrap the fish in cling film to form a cylinder

When fish is wrapped, place in the fridge to relax and cool down

Top and tail the leeks and slice down the middle

Remove the outside leaves and keep the insides

Blanch in boiling water then place in ice-cold water – this will keep the colour when cooking

Wrap the fish in the leek and set aside

Cut into 160g portions

Steam the hake gently for 7-8 minutes, using a temperature probe to make sure the core is at 42°C

FOR THE CHARRED SPRING ONIONS

1 bunch spring onions

Olive oil

Salt and pepper to season

Blanch the spring onions in boiling water for 30 seconds then plunge into ice-cold water to refresh

Drain and pat dry

Drizzle in olive oil and cut in half

Add to a really hot pan and cook until charred

Season to taste

FOR THE SAVOY CABBAGE PURÉE

1 savoy cabbage

70g butter

Remove the outer leaves of the cabbage and discard

Thinly slice the savoy

Melt the butter in a pan, when foaming add the savoy

Coat in the butter and soften

FOR THE SWEET AND SOUR WASABI PURÉE

100g wasabi purée

150g palm sugar

100g vinegar

Dried wasabi and watercress for garnish

Place the wasabi paste, palm sugar and vinegar in a small saucepan and boil until all dissolved

Garnish with dried wasabi and watercress

This is extremely powerful so only use a little

FOR THE PARSLEY OIL

200g parsley

300ml sunflower oil

Salt

Blanch parsley for 1 minute in boiling water

Refresh in iced water

Pat dry and transfer to a blender

Add oil and blend on full power until smooth

Place blender jug in freezer for 10 minutes to cool

Blend for 30 seconds and repeat this five times

Season to taste

SMOKED SPRING RISOTTO, PEA, HADDOCK, CHIVE

TASTE PROFILE:

This smoked haddock risotto is not like traditional risottos laced in butter and Parmesan, but instead a lighter approach softened by the crème fraîche and underlying smoked fish tones.

Serves: 6

Sweet: 0 1 2 3 4
Sour: 0 1 2
Bitter: 0
Salty: 0 1 2 3 4 5 6
Umami: 0 1 2 3 4

FOR THE RISOTTO BASE

250g arborio rice

6 shallots, finely diced

3 garlic cloves, puréed

100ml white wine

300ml fish stock

In a heavy-based saucepan melt the butter and add the finely diced shallots and garlic

Cook for 20 minutes on a low heat until soft and translucent

Pour in the arborio rice and stir, allow the rice to snap which means the starch is releasing

Add the white wine and reduce

Add the stock, ladle by ladle, cooking slowly, until the rice is al dente

FOR THE HADDOCK

3 sides smoked haddock

3 shallots

6 cloves

3 bay leaves

Small bunch chervil

1 stick lemongrass

1.5 litres milk

Stud the shallots with bay leaves and cloves

Pour the milk into a large saucepan

Add all ingredients

Lightly poach the fish in the saucepan for 6-7 minutes

Remove fish and pick into large chunks

Ensure there are no bones

FOR THE GARNISH

Chopped chives

Crème fraîche

Fresh spring peas

Parmesan

Picked chervil

Salt and pepper to season

Warm the risotto in a saucepan

Finish with crème fraîche, chives, peas and Parmesan

Add fish and let the residual heat of risotto warm the fish through but do not overcook the fish

Season to taste and garnish with fresh chervil or other herbs of your choosing

SEA BASS, CEPS & ENDIVE

TASTE PROFILE:

Sea bass is a meaty fish which needs meaty garnishes to stand up to it. Bitter endive and roast cep mushrooms are in my eyes the perfect combination. With good fish comes precise cooking so use a probe to make sure temperatures are correct.

Serves: 6

Sweet:	0 1 2 3 4 5
Sour:	0
Bitter:	0 1 2 3 4 5 6 7 8 9
Salty:	0 1 2 3 4 5
Umami:	0 1 2 3 4 5 6 7 8

FOR THE SEA BASS

1 sea bass

Remove the scales then cut the fillets from the bone
Rinse the fish then pat dry or ask your fishmonger to do this
Cut into pieces weighing about 160g each
Place on a small tray lined with greaseproof paper
Cook in the oven at 130°C for 12 minutes checking with a temperature probe to ensure the fish reaches 42°C

FOR THE CEPS

4 large ceps
2 cloves garlic, crushed
4 sprigs thyme, chopped
10g soy sauce
50g butter
Olive oil
Salt and pepper to season

Cut 3 of the ceps in half
In an ovenproof saucepan melt the butter with the crushed garlic and chopped thyme
When butter is golden brown add the ceps, cut side down, to get a nice colouring
Place in the oven at 160°C for 10 minutes
Once cooked remove from the oven and turn the ceps over
Tip the pan to move all the melted butter to one side
Add the soy and baste the mushroom in the soy butter
Slice the remaining cep very thinly, brush with olive oil, season and use to garnish the plate

FOR THE CHICKEN SAUCE

1 large onion
1 large carrot
½ head celery
½ clove garlic
1 sprig thyme
Splash white wine vinegar
100ml white wine
1kg chicken wings, roasted
1 litre chicken stock
50ml veal reduction (see basics)
3 tomatoes
3 flat cap mushrooms
Soy sauce

Caramelise the onion, carrot, celery, garlic and thyme
Add white wine vinegar and reduce until evaporated
Add white wine and reduce until it reaches a syrup-like consistency
Add the chicken stock and roasted chicken wings
Bring to a boil, skim, then simmer
Add tomatoes and flat cap mushrooms and simmer for 2 hours, skimming regularly
Pass the stock through a fine sieve into a clean saucepan
Add the veal reduction and reduce on a rolling boil until sauce consistency is reached
Roast the remaining chicken wings and add to the passed stock with the thyme, and let sit for 30 minutes
Add soy sauce for flavour
Pass through a fine sieve into suitable container
Chill

FOR THE RED ENDIVE

1 head endive
350ml chicken sauce

Remove each leaf from the head of endive
Bring the chicken sauce to the boil and remove from the heat then wilt the endive in the sauce

FOR THE ARTICHOKE PURÉE

1 lemon
8 large globe artichokes
60ml olive oil
650ml white wine
4 cloves garlic
3 sprigs thyme
Salt and pepper to season

Prepare the artichokes by peeling off the outer leaves, trimming the stalk, cut in half and scoop out the choke
Slice into quarters and place in a bowl of lemon water, this will stop them going brown. Pat dry before use
Add olive oil to a saucepan
Add the artichokes and sauté for 3 minutes
Add white wine and bring to the boil
Reduce by half then top with water
Add garlic, thyme and season
Top with a cartouche
Simmer slowly for 15 minutes then strain when tender
Blitz to a purée, adding a tablespoon of the liquid if needed to make a smooth consistency

TURBOT, PAK CHOI, COURGETTE, BASIL, SOY SAUCE

Serves: 6

TASTE PROFILE:

Turbot lightly cured before cooking sweetens the flavour by removing the moisture. It works really well with soy sauce and shiso.

Sweet:	⓪①❷❸❹
Sour:	⓪❶
Bitter:	⓪①❷❸❹❺❻
Salty:	⓪①❷❸❹❺
Umami:	⓪①❷❸❹❺❻❼

FOR THE TURBOT

1 side large turbot

75g table salt

75g caster sugar

50g sliced lemon zest, no pith

200ml extra virgin olive oil

Remove the skin

Trim off all the blood line

Combine salt, sugar and lemon zest

Rub the fish with the mix, slightly less around the tail area

Leave for 14 minutes then slice a thin piece, wash and taste to see ensure it is cured

If not cured then leave for a further 5-10 minutes

When cured wash the fish, being careful not to damage the flesh and pat dry

Pan-fry one side only

Cook the fish until the core temp is 42°C, checking with a temperature probe

FOR THE PICKLED PAK CHOI

1 head pak choi

100ml Amazu pickling liquid (see basics)

Remove the leaves and add the them to the Amazu pickling liquid

FOR THE ROAST PAK CHOI

1 head pak choi

Remove the leaves and roast them in a little olive oil allowing them to burn lightly

FOR THE SHISO LEAVES

1 bunch green shiso leaves (shiso is available from good oriental stores)

Vegetable oil for frying

Salt and pepper to season

Crisp the leaves in a pan with a little vegetable oil

Season and pat dry

FOR THE DRESSING

30ml quality soy sauce, such as Yamasa

FOR THE COURGETTE AND BASIL PURÉE

5 courgettes

1 bunch basil

50ml olive oil

5 cloves garlic

Peel the courgettes, keeping only the peel

Finely chop the peel

Pick the basil

Add olive oil to a large saucepan, add the garlic and courgette peel

Cook until golden brown then add the basil and blend

HALIBUT, OYSTERS, OCTOPUS, CUCUMBER

TASTE PROFILE:
A very true dish with nowhere to hide; sweet crispy oysters with buttery halibut and tender octopus all brought back to the sea with vibrant sea herbs.

Sweet: 0 1 2 3 4
Sour: 0 1 2 3 4
Bitter: 0
Salty: 0 1 2 3 4 5 6
Umami: 0

FOR THE OCTOPUS

1 octopus
100ml olive oil

Boil the octopus whole for 1 hour 45 minutes with the olive oil
When cooked, remove from the heat and place in ice cold water to chill down
Using a small knife remove outside skin keeping suckers intact
Thinly slice the octopus 'carpaccio' style
Lay on greaseproof paper

FOR THE HALIBUT

1kg halibut
Vegetable oil
Knob butter
Salt and pepper to season

Remove from bone, remove skin and cut into equal size portions of 160g or ask your fishmonger to do this
Season the fish then in add a little vegetable oil to a hot frying pan and place the halibut presentation side down
Turn off the heat and sit in the pan for 8 minutes letting the residual heat cook the fish through
Add a knob of butter and turn the heat back on
When the butter is golden brown turn the fish to warm the otherside then serve immediately

FOR THE OYSTERS

12 oysters
200ml Muscat wine
200ml fish stock
1 stick lemongrass
2 kaffir lime leaves
3 large parsley stalks
1 lemon
10g Maldon salt

Shuck the oysters
Combine all ingredients, except the oysters, in a saucepan and bring to the boil
Remove from heat
When temperature reaches 70°C add the oysters and slowly poach for 3-4 minutes

FOR THE PICKLED CUCUMBER

400ml water
100ml Sauternes wine
80g white wine vinegar
30g sugar
10g salt
10g dill
Small pinch of jasmine in a muslin bag
12 peppercorns
4 bay leaves
Sprig fresh mint
2 small cucumbers

Place all ingredients, except cucumber and mint, into a saucepan and bring to a simmer
Remove from heat and allow to cool, then chill in the fridge
Peel cucumber and add to the cold pickling liquid along with the mint
Leave for 20 minutes to infuse

FOR THE OYSTER BEIGNET

12 oysters
100g flour
100g breadcrumbs
100g egg whites

Shuck the oysters and remove the juice
Pané by dusting in flour, then dip into the beaten egg whites and then place into the breadcrumbs
Deep-fry at 180°C for 1 minute or until golden brown

FOR THE SEA VEGETABLES

Sea aster
Sea purslane
Raw oyster leaves
Chervil
Samphire
Knob of butter

I've suggested a few of my favourite sea vegetables but you can use any you prefer
Lightly blanch the vegetables in 100ml water with a knob of butter, then dress the plate with the vegetables

SASHIMI – SALMON, TUNA, SEA BASS, SCALLOPS

TASTE PROFILE:

Japanese food is something I always love to eat because of its uncomplicated approach and full flavour. Using fresh fish is extremely important in this dish but there's no strict guideline of which sauce goes with which fish – just play around and see what you prefer.

Serves: 8

Sweet:	⓪①②③④⑤⑥⑦
Sour:	⓪①②③④⑤⑥⑦
Bitter:	⓪①②③④⑤
Salty:	⓪①②③④⑤⑥⑦
Umami:	⓪①②③④⑤⑥⑦⑧

FOR THE SASHIMI

200g salmon
200g scallops
200g tuna
200g sea bass

Thinly slice each piece of fish

FOR THE SOY DRESSING

100g soy sauce
2 limes, juiced
½ tsp fresh ginger, finely chopped
50ml olive oil

Mix ingredients together
Pour over sliced fish and serve immediately

FOR THE YUZU DRESSING

140g grapeseed oil
50g soy sauce
90g yuzu juice
1 tsp fresh ground black pepper
2 cloves garlic, finely chopped

Mix ingredients together
Pour over sliced fish and serve immediately

FOR THE SPICY LEMON DRESSING

50g grapeseed oil
45g lemon juice
20g soy sauce
Pinch salt
Pinch black pepper
Pinch cayenne pepper
1 clove garlic, finely chopped

Mix ingredients together
Pour over sliced fish and serve immediately

FOR THE JALAPENO

140g grape seed oil
60g rice wine vinegar
2 cloves garlic, puréed
20g jalepenos, julienne

Mix ingredients together
Pour over sliced fish and serve immediately

COD CHEEKS, APPLE, SCRAPS, PEAS

TASTE PROFILE:

This is my take on fish and chips – without the chips!
Instead of battering and deep frying the cod cheeks,
we garnish with scraps of batter which have been
poured into the fryer and serve with fresh peas, pea
purée and acidic apple. Delicious.

Serves: 8

Taste	Level
Sweet:	0 1 **2**
Sour:	0 1 2 3 4
Bitter:	0
Salty:	0 1 2 3 4 5 6
Umami:	0 1 2 3 4

FOR THE COD CHEEKS

500g cod cheeks
100g salt
1 pinch garam masala
1 tbsp vegetable oil

Prepare the cod cheeks by removing excess sinew
Sprinkle with salt and leave for 7 minutes
Wash the salt off the cheeks and pat dry
Sprinkle with the garam masala
In a shallow pan add the vegetable oil
Pan-fry the cod cheeks for 1½ minutes each side
When golden brown remove from heat
Rest for 2 minutes

FOR THE PEA PURÉE

2 shallots
50g butter
100ml chicken stock
70ml cream
200g peas
Salt and pepper to season

Thinly slice shallots
In a saucepan add butter and the sliced shallots
Cook until translucent
Add the chicken stock and cream
Reduce slightly
Add peas and blitz
Season to taste
Pass through a fine sieve

FOR THE SCRAPS

100g cornflour
100g plain flour
200ml ice cold sparkling water
1 egg white
Vegetable oil for deep-frying
Salt and pepper to season

Combine plain flour and cornflour together with the
egg white and whisk
Add the sparkling water while slowly whisking gently
Heat the vegetable oil to 170°C
Using a spoon, drizzle the batter into the oil
When golden brown, remove and season

FOR THE APPLE GARNISH

1 Granny Smith apple

Thinly slice and cut into matchsticks

PICKED CRAB, WATERMELON, SWEETCORN

TASTE PROFILE:

Roasted watermelon and freshly picked white crab is a match made in heaven. Serving with the classic garnish of avocado makes it even more acidic and an extremely colourful dish to look at.

Serves: 6

Sweet:	⓪①❷❸❹
Sour:	⓪①❷❸❹
Bitter:	⓪①❷
Salty:	⓪①❷❸
Umami:	⓪①❷❸❹❺

FOR THE MAYONNAISE

2 large egg yolks

½ tsp Dijon mustard

100ml vegetable oil

10ml white wine vinegar

½ lemon, juiced

Add egg yolks, mustard and vinegar and lemon to a small food mixer with the whisk attachment, and whisk

While whisking, slowly pour in oil

The mixture should be thick and creamy

FOR THE CRAB

2 large, freshly cooked crabs

150g mayonnaise

Pinch paprika

Twist off the claws and hit with the back of a heavy knife to crack then remove the meat. Keep the shells to make a crab sauce or velouté

Pick out all of the remaining white crabmeat

Thoroughly check the meat and discard any trace of crab shell

Add the mayonnaise and a pinch of paprika

FOR THE AVOCADO PURÉE

2 ripe avocados

1 lime, juiced

1 tbsp crème fraîche

Halve the avocados, peel and then remove the stone

Blitz with the lime and crème fraîche to a purée

FOR THE SWEETCORN PURÉE

300g fresh sweetcorn

50ml reduced chicken stock

50ml double cream

Knob of butter

Salt

Add butter to a frying pan and toast the corn until golden

Add chicken stock and cream

Reduce until sweetcorn is fully cooked

Blitz to make purée

Pass through a sieve to remove all lumps

Season with salt

FOR THE WATERMELON

1 small watermelon

Cut the watermelon into sticks 1cm x 1cm x 5cm

Lightly oil a pan and roast on all 4 sides

Remove from heat

ORKNEY HAND DIVED SCALLOPS, CHICKEN, CANNELLONI BEANS, SHITAKE MUSHROOMS

Serves: 6

TASTE PROFILE:

Scallops with confit meat is a perfect match, even more so when adding the mushrooms and white beans. I love this dish and it's a regular on my menu.

Sweet: 0 1 2 3 4 5 6 7
Sour: 0 1 2 3 4 5 6
Bitter: 0 1 2 3 4
Salty: 0 1 2 3 4
Umami: 0 1 2 3 4 5 6

FOR THE SCALLOPS

3 scallops per portion
Pomace oil for frying
1 tsp Maldon sea salt
Knob of butter
½ lemon, juiced

Shuck the scallops by slipping a knife in the right fold of the shell

Run the knife along the top shell

Remove the scallop from the bottom of the shell using a soup spoon

Gently remove the outer sack and discard then gently wash the scallop in iced water and dry

To serve, place a frying pan on a medium heat with a touch of pomace oil

Season the presentation side with Maldon salt

Place the scallops in a pan, presentation side up

Cook slowly until golden brown

When golden brown, turn scallops, add butter and baste

Finish with lemon juice

Remove from pan and serve immediately

FOR THE CHICKEN LEG

2 chicken legs
500g duck fat
½ bulb garlic
1 bay leaf
1 sprig thyme
1 sprig rosemary
Salt

In a saucepan heat the duck fat to 60°C

Add the garlic, bay leaf, thyme and rosemary to the pan

Raise the temperature to 80°C and add the chicken legs

When the bone can easily be removed from the chicken, remove the saucepan from heat and allow to cool

To remove the legs from the duck fat, bring it to room temperature

Remove the meat from the chicken legs and discard the skin and bones and season to taste

FOR THE SHITAKE CRISPS

50g shitake mushrooms
Salt and pepper to season
Olive oil

Thinly slice the mushrooms and cook in a little olive oil until crisp

Season with salt and pepper

FOR THE GARNISH

Mustard frills
Truffle
White beans
Chicken sauce
Dried mushroom

SCALLOPS, APPLES, HAZELNUTS

TASTE PROFILE:

The scallops should only be cooked on one side – make sure they are golden brown before coming off the heat. Adding burnt apple purée and acidic fresh apple brings the scallops alive.

Sweet:	0 1 2 3 4 5 6
Sour:	0 1 2 3 4
Bitter:	0 1 2 3 4 5 6
Salty:	0 1 2 3 4
Umami:	0 1 2 3 4

FOR THE SCALLOPS

3 scallops per portion
Oil for frying
1 tsp Maldon sea salt
Knob of butter
1 lemon, juiced

Shuck the scallops by running a knife along the top shell
Remove the scallop from the bottom of the shell using a soup spoon
Remove the outer sack with your fingers and discard
Quickly plunge the scallops in iced water and pat dry
Place a frying pan on a medium heat with a touch of oil
Season the presentation side with Maldon sea salt
Place the scallops in a frying pan, presentation side up
Cook until golden brown then add the butter and baste
Finish with lemon juice
Remove from the pan and serve immediately

FOR THE APPLE PICKLE

2 apples
300ml water
100ml Muscat wine
50g white wine vinegar
30g sugar
10g salt
10g fresh mint

Slice the apples on a mandoline
Place all the ingredients, except the apple and mint into a saucepan and bring to a simmer
Remove from heat and add the apple
Leave for 5 minutes then add the mint
Leave to cool then place in a fridge to marinate for 24 hours

FOR THE VANILLA APPLE

2 Granny Smith apples, finely diced
1 vanilla pod
½ lemon
50g sugar
100g water

Add all ingredients, except the apple into a small saucepan
Bring to the boil then remove from heat
Infuse for 24 hours
Finely dice the apples and place into cold syrup
Leave for a further 12 hours

FOR THE BURNT APPLE PURÉE FOR THE PLATE

4 Granny smith apples

Quarter apples
Place in a small baking tray, lined with tin foil
Place in oven at 180°C for 30-35 minutes or until dark coloured
Allow to cool
Blitz until smooth then pass through a sieve

FOR THE BURNT APPLE PURÉE TURNOVERS

50g burnt apple purée
Lemon juice

Combine with a squeeze of lemon and pipe on the plate

FOR THE JASMINE OIL

2 stalks lemongrass
½ vanilla pod
1 kaffir lime leaf
125ml olive oil
½ tsp jasmine

Combine all to a food blender
Blitz
Pass through a sieve
Leave for no more than 3 days

FOR THE GARNISH

Hazelnuts, lightly toasted
Pea shoots
Chervil

MONKFISH, BURNT CAULIFLOWER, BABY GEM, ROAST GARLIC, PARSLEY VELOUTÉ

TASTE PROFILE:

Monkfish is a bold fish which can take a lot of flavours so serving with a white bean purée, pickled baby gems and bursts of caviar is a great way of doing the fish justice.

Sweet:	0 1 2 **3 4 5 6**	
Sour:	0 1 2 **3 4 5 6**	
Bitter:	0 1 2 **3 4**	
Salty:	0 1 2 **3 4**	
Umami:	0 **1 2**	

FOR THE MONKFISH

2kg monkfish

Remove the monkfish tail and remove the skin

Trim off all the grey blood line

Combine salt, sugar and lemon zest

Rub the cure around the monkfish

After 11 minutes, wash and taste to see whether it is cured enough then pat dry

Pan-fry in vegetable oil until golden brown and place in the oven at 120°C for 6 minutes

Remove from the pan and allow to rest for 5 minutes before slicing

FOR THE VELOUTÉ

2 bulbs garlic

300ml chicken stock

200g parsley juice

50g cream

100g butter, diced

30ml Amazu pickling liquid

Salt

Roast the garlic until golden

Add to chicken stock and reduce slightly

Add the cream and bring back to the boil then season with salt

Add the parsley juice and Amazu

Blend with a handblender while adding the butter

FOR THE PICKLED GEM LETTUCE

2 baby gem lettuce

30ml Amazu pickling liquid

Remove the leaves from the baby gem's then pour over the Amazu pickling liquid and leave to sit for 10 minutes in a bowl

FOR THE CAULIFLOWER PURÉE

1 large cauliflower, or use cauliflower scraps

65g butter

Splash single cream

100ml dark chicken stock (see basics)

Salt

1 lemon, juice

Cut the cauliflower into 1 inch thick pieces

Melt the butter in a frying pan

Fry the cauliflower mixing so butter it foams

Cook until cauliflower is golden brown

Add chicken stock

Add a splash of cream

Pass through a sieve and blitz with a handblender

Season with salt and squeeze of lemon

FOR THE BORLOTTI BEANS

100g beans

200ml chicken stock (see basics)

Knob of butter

Blanch the beans, leaving a little bite to them

Allow to cool then remove the skins

In a saucepan cook the beans in a little chicken stock then reduce and add butter

FOR THE DRESSING

Caviar

Amazu pickling liquid

FOR THE GARNISH

Watercress

Diced bread croutons in garlic

SALMON, PEAS, DILL

TASTE PROFILE:

I won British Chef of the Year with this dish.
The unusual approach of pairing salmon and cold peas
on one dish works well due to the freshness of the
peas and the precision cooked salmon.

Serves: 6

Sweet: ⓿❶❷❸❹❺❻
Sour: ⓿
Bitter: ⓿❶❷❸❹
Salty: ⓿❶❷❸❹
Umami: ⓿❶❷❸

FOR THE SALMON

1kg side salmon

75g table salt

75g caster sugar

Fennel pollen, for dusting

2 lemon, zest

50ml extra virgin olive oil

Remove the salmon from the bone and remove the pin
bones from the salmon, or ask your fishmonger to do this

Remove the skin and trim off all the grey blood line

Next, combine the salt, sugar and lemon zest

Rub both sides of the fish with this mix apply slightly
less of the cure around the tail area

After 2 hours wash off the cure and pat dry

Remove the salmon belly and keep the presentation part

Sprinkle both sides with the fennel pollen

Cut the salmon fillet into portions

Bring the salmon to room temperature then place each
salmon fillet into a saucepan of extra virgin olive oil

Place the saucepan on a low heat and use a probe to
make sure you get a perfect cooking temperature of
45°C and cook for 15 minutes

FOR THE DILL OIL

4 bunches dill

300ml vegetable oil

Pick the dill and blanch in salted water for 7 seconds

Refresh in iced water

Lay half out on a tray and leave to dry slightly

Add this to a blender, add the vegetable oil and blend for
1 minute

Place into the fridge to cool

FOR THE DRIED DILL & DILL POWDER

2 bunches dill

Pinch of sea salt

Lay out the dill sprigs on a tray

Place in an oven at 100°C for 30 minutes to dry out

Season with a little sea salt

To make the dill powder, rub the remaining dried dill
using your fingers

FOR THE PEA PANNA COTTA

2½ gelatine leaves

200g peas

250ml water

50g cream

Salt and pepper to season

Blend the peas with 250ml water until smooth

Soak the gelatine in iced water

Bring the cream to the boil and dissolve the gelatine

Add to the pea liquid to the cream

Season with salt and pepper whilst still warm

Place in fridge to set for about 1 hour

FOR THE APPLE PICKLE

2 apples

10g fresh mint

400ml water

100ml Sauternes wine

40g rice vinegar

30g sugar

10g salt

10g dill

12 peppercorns

4 bay leaves

Cut the apples into ½cm pieces

Place all ingredients, except the apple and mint, into a saucepan and bring to a gentle simmer

Remove from the heat and add apple

Leave for 5 minutes then add the mint

Leave to cool then place in the fridge to marinate for 24 hours

FOR THE SWEET AND SOUR WASABI

180g sugar

180ml vinegar

400ml water

130g palm sugar

70g wasabi powder

50ml stock syrup (see basics)

9g agar

Boil sugar and vinegar to a syrup

Add water and palm sugar, cook to dissolve

Add the wasabi to the water and cook out to a paste

Add the syrup to the wasabi

Bring to the boil

Add the agar and sugar solution

Cook for 30 seconds then set in container

Leave for 24 hours

FOR THE PEAS

200g peas

200g dill oil

Salt & pepper for seasoning

Shell peas

Add dill oil

Season to taste

FOR THE GARNISH

Seasoned dry dill sprigs

Black caviar

Dill powder

SCOTTISH SALMON, SMOKED OIL, ENGLISH GOAT'S CHEESE, BEETROOT

TASTE PROFILE:

The cured and confit salmon is melt in the mouth and so full of flavour and adding the smoked oil takes it to a new level.

	Scale
Sweet:	0 1 2
Sour:	0
Bitter:	0 1 2 3 4
Salty:	0 1 2 3 4
Umami:	0 1 2 3

FOR THE SALMON

1kg side salmon
30g table salt
30g caster sugar
1 lemon, zest finely sliced
200ml extra virgin olive oil

Remove the salmon from the bone
Pin bone the salmon
Remove the skin from the salmon
Trim off all the grey blood line
Combine salt, sugar and zest of lemons
Rub both sides of the fish with this mix, slightly less around the tail area
After 90 minutes, carefully wash the fish, taking care not to damage the flesh then pat dry
Cut into 65g portions
Place each portion into warm extra virgin olive oil
Cook at 45°C for 15 minutes on a low heat in a saucepan
Remove from oil and place on a tray with a cloth
Place in a container and put in the fridge to chill
To serve drizzle with a little smoked oil

FOR THE SMOKED OIL

100ml olive oil
1 piece coal

Heat a piece of coal on a gas burner or hob
Pour some olive oil into a metal container
When the coal glows red, carefully remove and drop into the olive oil, cover immediately with a lid
Leave for 30 minutes or until cold to infuse the oil
This smoked oil will last 6 months

FOR THE ROAST SHALLOTS

3 banana shallots
15ml olive oil
2 sprigs thyme
Salt and pepper to season

Finely dice the shallots
Add olive oil, diced shallots and thyme in a small saucepan and cook until translucent
Season with salt and pepper then allow to cool

FOR THE WHIPPED GOAT'S CHEESE

Roast shallots
300g soft goat's cheese
2 tbsp honey
Salt and pepper to season

When roast shallots are cold, combine all ingredients and beat until smooth

FOR THE BEETROOT

3 baby beetroot
100ml Amazu pickling liquid

Thinly slice beetroot
Pour over warm Amazu and leave for 24 hours to infuse

FOR THE APPLE PICKLE

2 apples
200g rice wine vinegar
200g sugar
18g salt
1 lemon, juiced
1 sprig mint

Ball the apples in to ½cm balls
Mix the rice wine vinegar, sugar and salt in a saucepan and bring to gentle simmer then remove from the heat
Add then apple, mint and lemon juice
Leave for 2 hours to infuse

FOR THE BEETROOT FILLED CYLINDERS

1 whole beetroot

Place a whole beetroot in cold water
Bring to the boil and cook until tender, this usually takes around 3 hours
When cooked allow to cool
Cut a cylinder with a small cutter, then use an apple corer and remove the centre to make a tube
Fill the tube with the goat's cheese and shallot mixture

FOR THE GARNISH

Picked leaves
Red chard
Flowers

MEAT

VENISON, PEAR, CELERY, MUSTARD

TASTE PROFILE:

Roe venison is one of my favourite types of venison due to its smaller size and sweet game flavour. Serving it with roasted pear and bitter celery creates a contrast that makes a perfectly balanced dish.

Serves: 6

Sweet: ⓪①②③④
Sour: ⓪①②③④⑤
Bitter: ⓪①②③
Salty: ⓪①②③④
Umami: ⓪①②③

FOR THE VENISON

1 saddle roe deer venison

3 cloves garlic

Small bunch thyme

Butter

Salt and pepper to season

Vegetable oil for frying

Remove the loins from the bone and trim off all the sinew or ask your butcher to do this

In a heavy-based pan, add a little vegetable oil, when hot add the venison and seal on each side until golden brown

Add the butter, thyme, garlic and seasoning and baste the venison

Place in an oven at 140°C for 9 minutes and then remove and rest for 6 minutes

Carve and season to taste

FOR THE PEAR

2 pears

Knob of butter

Black pepper for seasoning

Cut the pears in half and trim off the edges

Pan-fry in a little butter until both sides are golden brown

Season with fresh cracked black pepper

FOR THE BRAISED CELERY

8 sticks celery hearts

200ml chicken stock

50g butter

Bring the stock and butter to the boil and remove from heat

Add the celery and cook slowly for about 1 minute

FOR THE MUSTARD DRESSING

10g mustard seeds

1 stick celery, finely diced

80ml olive oil

35ml rice wine vinegar

10ml soy sauce

Peel and finely dice the celery

Warm the olive oil and add the celery

Cook until clear and tender

In a saucepan of boiling water add the mustard seeds and boil for 3 minutes

Drain and rinse until water runs clear

When celery is cooked add the rice wine, vinegar and soy

Finish with the mustard seeds

DEER, CAULIFLOWER, PEAR, SZECHUAN PEPPER

Serves: 6

TASTE PROFILE:

Game and bitter chocolate work very well together, but by adding the soy sauce and sherry vinegar to the chocolate an amazing flavour combination is created.

Sweet: 0 1 2 3 4
Sour: 0 1 2 3 4 5 6 7
Bitter: 0 1 2 3 4 5 6
Salty: 0 1 2 3
Umami: 0 1 2 3 4 5 6 7

FOR THE VENISON

1 venison saddle
4 sprigs thyme
3 bay leaves
50ml olive oil
1 clove garlic, crushed

Debone the venison saddle and cut into portions
Marinade in the herbs, oil and crushed garlic
Pan-fry until golden brown
Season and cook in the oven for 4 minutes
Rest for 8 minutes then place back in a pan with foaming butter to warm up
Carve to serve

FOR THE VENISON SEASONING

5g juniper berries, very finely chopped
3 cep mushrooms, very finely chopped
4 Szechuan peppercorns, crushed
1 lime, zested and very finely chopped
1 tsp salt

Chop all the ingredients to a very fine dice
Dry out in the oven at 100°C for 1 hour
Pass through tea strainer to make a powder
Combine and use as a seasoning

FOR THE CHOCOLATE

250g 70% cocoa dark chocolate
40ml olive oil
40ml soy
40ml sherry vinegar

Melt the chocolate
Whisk in the rest of the ingredients

FOR THE PICKLED CAULIFLOWER

1 cauliflower
200ml rice vinegar
200g sugar
18g salt

Place all the ingredients, except the cauliflower, into a pan and bring to a simmer
Remove from heat and chill
Thinly slice the florets
Place cauliflower in the liquid
Leave to stand for 2 hours

FOR THE CAULIFLOWER PURÉE

1kg cauliflower scraps
130g butter
100ml dark chicken stock (see basics)
Splash cream
Salt to season
½ lemon, juiced

Cut the cauliflower up to 1 inch thick pieces
Melt butter in frying pan
Fry the cauliflower, mixing so the butter is frothed
Cook until golden brown
Add chicken stock
Add a splash of cream
Pass through a sieve and blitz with a handblender
Season with salt and a squeeze of lemon to taste

FOR THE GARNISH

Micro cauliflower
Raw sliced pears

ASHED BEEF FILLET, GARLIC, BARLEY, GRELOT, MARROWS

Serves: 6

TASTE PROFILE:

Beef coated in ash is one of my signature dishes, and cooking it with burnt herbs brings a molasses taste to the meat which sets off the dish perfectly.

Sweet:	❶❷❸
Sour:	❶❷❸❹❺❻❼
Bitter:	❶❷❸❹❺❻❼
Salty:	❶❷❸❹❺
Umami:	❶❷❸❹❺❻❼❽❾

FOR THE BEEF FILLET

1 centre cut beef fillet

FOR THE HERB ASH

3 bunches parsley

1 bunch mint

1 bunch dill

2 bunches chervil

Pick all the herb leaves then grill until charred black

Allow to go cold then blitz to a fine powder

Pass through a tea strainer

Trim any fat and sinew from the beef fillet

Sprinkle the fillet in the herb powder until totally covered

Tightly wrap in cling film

Put a large saucepan of water on the stove, place a tea towel in the saucepan and put a temperature probe into the water

Cook the cling-filmed meat at 65°C for 40 minutes

Remove meat from the bath and leave to cool to room temperature

Reheat in the saucepan of water at 65°C for 25 minutes

FOR THE SMOKED OIL

250ml extra virgin olive oil

1 piece of coal

Place oil in an old pan with a lid

Burn coals until roasting hot

Blow out coals

Drop them into the oil

Place lid on

Leave for 15 minutes

Pass through a coffee strainer

FOR THE PARSLEY PURÉE

125g picked flat-leaf parsley

Salt and pepper to season

Blanch the parsley in salted water

Refresh in ice-cold water

Lightly squeeze and blend until smooth adding a couple of ice cubes if needed

Measure out 450g of the parsley purée liquid

Pass through fine sieve

Reserve for when needed

FOR THE GARLIC PURÉE

250g peeled garlic

½ litre full fat milk

Salt and pepper to season

Bring the milk to boil

Blanch garlic for 30 seconds in the milk

Remove the garlic

Allow to cool then repeat seven times

Season with salt and pepper

Blend to a purée

FOR THE PARSELY GARLIC PURÉE

Combine 200g parsley purée with 100g garlic purée

Season with salt and pepper

Place in squeezy bottle

FOR THE PEARL BARLEY

200g pearl barley
500ml chicken stock
Salt and pepper to season

Soak barley in water overnight
Rinse and drain
Bring barley and stock to boil
Simmer for 25 minutes
Reheat with white chicken stock when needed
Season to taste

FOR THE MARROWS

10 marrowbones, cut into 2cm pieces
100g salt
1 litre water
Flour for dusting
Egg, whisked
Panko breadcrumbs

Soak marrowbones for 24 hours in salted water
Remove marrow from bones
Using hot knife, dice into 2cm pieces
Pané by dusting the marrowbone firstly in flour, then egg and finally the breadcrumbs
Deep fry until golden allowing 5 pieces per portion

FOR THE WILD GARLIC

Handful wild garlic leaves
50g butter
75ml water

Melt the butter in the water to emulsify, stir, then cook the wild garlic in the butter emulsion

FOR THE PICKLED MUSHROOMS

100g girolle mushrooms
100ml Amuzu pickle liquid (see basics)

Warm pickle liquid and pour over the mushrooms
Cling film the container and let sit until they go cold

GARNISH

Red watercress

PRESSED OLD SPOT PORK, PINEAPPLE, HAZELNUTS AND CHEDDAR

Serves: 8

TASTE PROFILE:

My take on the classic ham and pineapple combination with variations of crispy and roasted pineapple balanced by the cheddar cheese cream.

Sweet:	⓪①②③④⑤
Sour:	⓪①②③④
Bitter:	⓪
Salty:	⓪①②③④⑤⑥
Umami:	⓪①②③④

FOR THE HAM HOCKS

2 unsmoked ham hocks

3 carrots

1 leek

½ head celery

5 shallots

10 peppercorns

3 bay leaves

1 bunch thyme

200ml white wine

1 bulb garlic

Soak ham hocks in water overnight then rinse in cold running water to refresh

Peel and cut the carrots, leek, celery and shallots into 1 inch thick pieces

Add to large saucepan with the ham hocks

Top with water, white wine, and the peppercorns, bay leaves, thyme and garlic

Slowly cook for 6 hours until meat is tender and falls from the bone

Once cooked remove from heat and let ham hocks relax in the liquid for an hour

Remove ham hocks from the stock

Pick the meat from the bone and reserve

Pass stock through a sieve and retain

TO MAKE THE TERRINE

50g duck fat

1 tbsp chervil, finely chopped

1 tbsp parsley, finely chopped

1 tsp thyme, finely chopped

Pinch mustard powder

Pinch cayenne pepper

1 banana shallot

Salt and pepper to season

Picked ham hocks

Line a terrine mould with triple-layered cling film

Cut shallots in half and roast in the oven

When roasted, blitz and pass through a fine sieve

Place the warm picked ham hock meat in a bowl

Melt the duck fat

Add all ingredients to the bowl

Season to taste

Place in the lined terrine mould and place a weight on top to press for 24 hours

FOR THE PINEAPPLE CARPACCIO

1 baby pineapple

1 tsp Szechuan pepper

1 lime, zested

10g mint

50ml sugar

75ml water

Place the Szechuan pepper, sugar and water in a saucepan and bring to boil

Peel baby pineapple

Slice very thinly on a mandoline or meat slicer

Cut each disk into a perfect circle

Remove liquid from heat

Add the mint and lime

Pour over pineapple

Leave to marinate for 24 hours

FOR THE CARAMELISED PINEAPPLE

150g small diced pineapple

50g sugar

Make a dry caramel by melting the sugar over a high-heat in a saucepan – try not to stir too often

Once the sugar is melted, quickly add the pineapple and caramelise

FOR THE CHEESE SAUCE

175g good cheddar

250g single cream

100g whole milk

Add the milk and cream to a saucepan then boil

Grate the cheese and add to a blender

Pour over the hot cream and blend on high for 2 minutes

FOR THE HAZELNUT PRALINE

50g hazelnuts, blanched

50g sugar

Blanch the hazelnuts by placing into boiling water for 10 seconds, remove, allow to cool slightly then rub in a clean tea towel to remove the skins

Make a dry caramel by melting the sugar over a high-heat in a saucepan – try not to stir too often

Crush hazelnuts, add to the dry caramel and toast

Pour on a silicone mat or greaseproof lined tray and roll thinly

Allow to cool and then break into pieces

FOR THE GARNISH

Pork skins

RIB-EYE BEEF, SAVOY CABBAGE, CARROTS

Serves: 6

TASTE PROFILE:

It's all about the meat with this dish, so make sure you buy good quality rib-eye, nothing less than 35 day aged with nice marbling. It pays off when eating.

Sweet: ⓿❶②③④
Sour: ⓿
Bitter: ⓿❶②③④⑤
Salty: ⓿❶②③④⑤⑥
Umami: ⓿

FOR THE RIB-EYE

400g beef rib-eye

Olive oil for frying

Cut the rib-eye into slices about 3 inches thick

In a hot pan add a little olive oil and seal the for 1 minute each side

Place in an oven at 140°C for 13 minutes then leave to rest for 5 minutes

Slice the meat into one inch slices then turn over

FOR THE SAVOY CABBAGE PURÉE

1 savoy cabbage

100ml chicken stock

70g butter

Salt and pepper to season

Remove the outer leaves of the cabbage and discard

Thinly slice the savoy

Melt the butter in a pan, add the savoy when foaming

Coat in the butter and soften

Add the chicken stock and reduce

Drain off the savoy and blend to a purée

Season to taste

FOR THE BABY CARROTS

1 bunch rainbow carrots

Peel and blanch the carrots in boiling water then refresh in ice-cold water

Cook the carrots in a griddle or frying pan

FOR THE ONION RINGS

1 large onion

100g cornfour

100g plain flour

1 egg white

200g sparkling water

Salt and pepper for seasoning

Thinly slice the onion

Make a batter by mixing the flours together with the egg white and slowly adding the ice-cold water

Flour the onion ring then dip in the batter

Deep fry until crispy

Season to taste

QUAIL, DATES, SOY

Serves: 6

TASTE PROFILE:

Quail is a delicious bird that can easily be overcooked, so always roast on a low heat to prevent this from happening. I serve this with my take on a teriyaki sauce, this brings extra sweetness, counter-balanced by the burnt onions.

Sweet: 0 1 2 3 4 5 6
Sour: 0 1 2 3
Bitter: 0 1 2 3 4
Salty: 0 1 2 3 4
Umami: 0 1 2 3 4 5 6 7 8

FOR THE QUAIL

6 quail

1 bunch thyme

2 garlic cloves

50g butter

Vegetable oil for frying

Salt and pepper to season

Trim the quail by removing the wishbone and excess fat

Seal very quickly in a hot pan with a little oil

Remove from the pan and cook in the oven at 120°C for 7 minutes

Let rest for 10 minutes

In the same pan add the butter, thyme and garlic

When the butter is golden brown, flash fry the quail in the butter, thyme and garlic

Season then carve off the bone

FOR THE CAULIFLOWER PURÉE

1 small cauliflower (or 500g cauliflower scraps)

65g butter

50ml dark chicken stock (see basics)

Splash double cream

Salt

Cut the cauliflower into 1 inch thick pieces

Melt the butter in a frying pan

Fry cauliflower while mixing so butter is frothed and cook until golden brown

Add the chicken stock

Add a splash of cream

Pass through a sieve, blitz and season to taste

FOR THE DATES

100g fresh dates

Butter

Remove the stones from the dates

Caramelise in a little butter in a small pan

Cook until the butter is golden brown

FOR THE SAUCE

20g ginger, grated

1 garlic clove, grated

100ml apple juice

100ml good soy sauce

100g palm sugar

Grate the ginger and garlic together

Add everything together in a saucepan and reduce by half over a medium heat

FOR THE GARNISH

Fresh apple, sliced

Red chard

PEAS AND HAM

TASTE PROFILE:

Peas and ham are classic components, and this dish is all about showcasing amazing ham with perfectly sweet peas. Invest in some Iberico Jamon for this dish – it's easy to find at most supermarkets and won't disappoint.

Serves: 6

Sweet:	⓪①②③④⑤⑥❼
Sour:	⓪①❷
Bitter:	⓪①②③❹
Salty:	⓪①②③④⑤❻
Umami:	⓪①②❸

FOR THE PEA MOUSSE

200g frozen peas

2 gelatine leaves

250ml water

150ml double cream

Salt and pepper to season

100ml parsley purée (see basics)

In a saucepan, soak the gelatine in cold water then bring to the boil and melt it

Add the peas and blend until smooth

Season to taste

Pass through a sieve then chill over ice until cool

Whip the cream to soft peaks

To the puréed peas, add the parsley purée and fold in the whipped cream

Place in the fridge to set

To serve, use a hot spoon and scoop a quenelle of the pea mousse on to the plate

FOR THE HAM

6 slices good quality Iberico Jamon

100g lardo, diced

Add the ham and diced lardo to the plate

FOR THE DILL OIL

1 bunch of dill

75ml vegetable oil

Salt and pepper to season

Pick the dill and blanch in boiling salted water for 7 seconds then refresh in iced water

Lay out the dill on a tray and leave to dry

Once dry add to a blender with the vegetable oil

Blend for 1 minute then place the blender jug in fridge for 10 minutes

Repeat the process 2 more times

Once blended cool instantly to preserve colour

Season to taste before serving

FOR THE PEAS

200g peas

50ml dill oil

Salt and pepper to season

Shell the peas

Add the dill oil then season to taste

FOR THE GARNISH

Pea shoots

Pea flowers

PORK BELLY, OCTOPUS, SQUID, MUSSEL CONSOMMÉ

TASTE PROFILE:

This dish has a huge Japanese influence with the soy sauce complementing the smoked mussel consommé, all brought together with the octopus and British pork. If you don't fancy curing the pork yourself, most butchers sell salted pork belly, so skip that step.

Sweet: 0 1 2 3 4 5
Sour: 0 1 2 3 4 5 6
Bitter: 0 1 2 3 4
Salty: 0 1 2 3 4 5 6
Umami: 0 1 2 3 4 5

CURING THE PORK BELLY

700g piece pork belly

75g salt

35g sugar

2 black peppercorns

1 litre water

1 bay leaf

1 sprig thyme

½ medium carrot, cut into 1 inch pieces

½ leek, white only, cut into 1 inch pieces

½ small onion, cut into 1 inch pieces

Mix the salt, sugar and peppercorns in a large container

Heat about 250ml of the water and add the dry mixture, stirring to dissolve to make a brine

Add the remaining water, vegetables and herbs

Chill the brine

Remove the skin from the pork belly and reserve

Add the pork belly to the brine and refrigerate overnight

Remove the pork from the brine and brush off the extra seasoning

COOKING THE PORK BELLY

1 brined pork belly

1 sprig thyme

1 bay leaf

5 peppercorns

300ml chicken stock

Place the pork in an oven safe dish with all remaining ingredients

Cook at 140°C for 4-5 hours

Once cooked, remove from oven and press overnight then refrigerate

Remove any excess fat from the top of the meat, leaving a thin layer of fat

Finish the pork belly by cutting it in straight-edged blocks

Roast on a high heat in a frying pan, skin-side down until crispy

FOR THE OCTOPUS

1 octopus

100ml olive oil

Remove tentacles from the octopus

Boil the octopus whole for 1 hour 45 minutes with the olive oil

When cooked, remove from the heat and place in ice cold water to chill down

Using a small knife remove outside skin keeping suckers intact

Individually portion into 6 inch pieces

Lay on grease proof paper until needed

FOR THE DULSE PICKLE

125g dulse, chopped

100ml water

25ml Sauterne wine

10ml white wine vinegar

7g sugar

½ tsp salt

3 peppercorns

1 bay leaf

Chop the dulse into 2cm pieces

Place all the ingredients, except the dulse, into a saucepan and bring to a gentle simmer

Remove from the heat and add the dulse

Allow to cool then place in the fridge to marinate for 24 hours

CONFIT LEMON

4 large un-waxed Italian lemons

100g caster sugar

5g salt

Cut the lemons into segments with the rind on

Mix with the sugar and salt

Wrap in tin foil and bake in the oven 40 minutes at 140°C

Chill in the fridge and then dice into chunks when ready to serve

FOR THE MUSSEL CONSOMMÉ

1 litre white wine

100ml vegetable oil

40ml dark soy

80ml mirin

Heat a wok until smoking

Add the vegetable oil and once smoking add a handful of mussels and smoke with a blowtorch

Once it stops smoking, add a splash of white wine

Cover with a lid until mussels are cooked and open

Repeat until you have used all the mussels

Add the remaining white wine

Once the mussel stock has smoked, pass through a fine sieve, add the dark soy and mirin and season to taste

Hang in coffee strainer overnight and do not force through

FOR THE GARNISH

Crispy pork skin

Sea herbs

GOAT SHEPHERD'S PIE

Serves: 5

TASTE PROFILE:

I like to use goat mince rather than lamb as it has a
better flavour and can be treated the same way. It's
finished with soy sauce and rice wine vinegar, making
for a full flavoured dish.

Sweet: ⓪①②③④⑤⑥⑦
Sour: ⓪①②
Bitter: ⓪①②
Salty: ⓪①②③④
Umami: ⓪①②③④⑤⑥⑦⑧

FOR THE GOAT RAGU

1kg minced goat shoulder

100ml vegetable oil

150g diced shallots

50g minced garlic

15g thyme leaf

50g tomato paste

500g tomatoes, peeled, seeded and roughly chopped

300ml chicken stock

60g soy sauce

75ml rice wine vinegar

Salt and pepper to season

Add the oil to a heavy-based pan and fry the mince

When caramelised add the diced shallots, garlic and
thyme then fry

Add the tomato paste and toast off

Add the fresh tomatoes and chicken stock

Simmer for around 1 hour ensuring liquid is reduced and
sticky

Remove from heat, add soy sauce and rice vinegar

Season to taste

FOR THE MASH

500g Charlotte potatoes

100g cream

70g butter

3 egg yolks

Salt and pepper to season

Wash potatoes and roast in the oven until golden

Pass through a fine sieve to remove every lump

Add cream, butter and egg yolks

Beat and season

GOAT SHOULDER, SHALLOTS, SHISO, CONSOMMÉ

Serves: 8

TASTE PROFILE:

This goat shoulder dish is perfect for when you're wanting good old fashioned comfort food. The ponzu chicken sauce elevates the flavours and really complements the goat.

Sweet: ⓿❶❷❸
Sour: ⓿❶❷❸❹❺❻
Bitter: ⓿❶❷❸❹❺
Salty: ⓿❶❷❸❹❺❻❼
Umami: ⓿❶❷❸❹❺❻❼❽

FOR THE GOAT SHOULDER

1 whole goat shoulder, bone in and including neck
12 heads garlic
Bunch fresh rosemary
Maldon salt
Olive oil

Place the shoulder in a saucepan with lid, deep enough to hold the shoulder and cover with olive oil
Chop the garlic and rosemary and add to the saucepan
Season to taste
Cover saucepan and place in oven for 5 hours at 130°C or until the bones feel as if they could be pulled out of the joint
Allow to chill naturally
Remove the meat and drain on a rack for 1 hour
Carefully remove the neck bone, shoulder blade and leg bone, which should come out easily
Pick off all the meat from the neck bone, shred and reserve

FOR THE GOAT RAGU

1kg shredded goat shoulder
100ml vegetable oil
150g diced shallots
50g minced garlic
15g thyme leaf
50g tomato paste
500g tomatoes, skinned, peeled and roughly chopped
300ml chicken stock
60g soy sauce
75ml rice wine vinegar

Add the oil to a heavy-based pan and fry the goat
When caramelised add the diced shallots, garlic and thyme and fry until golden
Stir in the tomato paste and cook for another 2 minutes
Then add the fresh tomatoes and chicken stock
Simmer for around 1 hour ensuring liquid is reduced and sticky
Remove from heat, add soy sauce and rice vinegar
Season to taste

FOR THE ONION OIL

50g chives
50g leek tops
50g spring onion tops
300ml sunflower oil
Salt

Place all ingredients in a blender and blend for 5 minutes
Chill then blend again for 5 minutes
Pass through muslin
Leave to rest in an upright container
Keep for a maximum of 5 days and remove oil from top not bottom

FOR THE CHICKEN SAUCE

1 large onion
1 large carrot
½ head celery
½ clove garlic
1 sprig thyme
Splash white wine vinegar
100ml white wine
1kg chicken wings, roasted
1 litre chicken stock
50ml veal reduction (see basics)
3 tomatoes
3 flat cap mushrooms
Soy sauce

Caramelise the onions, carrot, celery, garlic and thyme
Add white wine vinegar and reduce until evaporated
Add white wine and reduce until it reaches a syrup-like consistency
Add the chicken stock and roasted chicken wings
Bring to a boil, skim, then simmer
Add tomatoes and flat cap mushrooms and simmer for 2 hours, skimming regularly
Pass the stock through a fine sieve into a clean saucepan
Add the veal reduction and reduce on a rolling boil until sauce consistency is reached
Roast the remaining chicken wings and add to the passed stock with the thyme, and let sit for 30 minutes
Add soy sauce for flavour
Pass through a fine sieve into suitable container and chill

FOR THE CHICKEN BUTTER

600g chicken sauce, not reduced
300g beurre noisette (see basics)
50g ponzu
Salt and pepper to season

Whisk the butter into the chicken sauce
Finish with the ponzu
Season to taste

FOR THE SAUCE GARNISH

1 tsp baby capers
½ tsp diced shallots

Warm up the brown butter sauce
Finish with 1 tsp capers and ½ tsp diced shallots

FOR THE SHALLOT PURÉE

50 shallots, thinly sliced
120ml olive oil
150g butter
200ml dark chicken stock
100ml mirin (Japanese wine)
Salt

Thinly slice shallots
Add olive oil and butter to saucepan on high heat
Sweat shallots until soft and translucent
When moisture has evaporated reduce heat to low
Cook for 2 hours until shallots are golden and
caramelised
Add chicken stock
Deglaze and scrape off the bottom of the pan
Mix chicken stock and mirin
Reduce chicken stock slightly
Pass through sieve
Blend the shallots until smooth using liquid if needed
Season to taste

FOR THE CARAMELISED SHALLOTS

6 shallots
150ml rice wine vinegar
50ml maple syrup
50ml muscavado sugar
45g butter
Salt and black pepper to season

Peel the shallots whole, cut in half lengthwise then cut
into quarters lengthwise
Mix all other ingredients together
Pour over shallots
Place a damp cartouche on the shallots
Tin foil the saucepan
Cook at 160°C for 45 minutes
For service, caramelise on the plancher

FOR THE SHISO

Shiso leaves
Vegetable oil

Oil the shiso leaves
BBQ or grill until crisp
Remove and allow to cool then roughly rub to break up
Use to garnish the dish

FOR THE GARNISH

Garlic flowers

CHICKEN AND LOBSTER YELLOW CURRY

TASTE PROFILE:
Everything I love about Southeast Asia is right here. The yellow curry base can be made well in advance and lasts a long time, so is perfect for a quick meal. The chicken and lobster together is a wonderful combination.

Serves: 6

Sweet:	⓿❶❷❸❹
Sour:	⓿❶❷❸❹❺
Bitter:	⓿❶❷❸
Salty:	⓿❶❷❸❹❺❻
Umami:	⓿❶❷❸❹❺❻

FOR THE LOBSTER

2 litres water

Salt

100ml white wine vinegar

2 female lobsters of the same size

Bring a large pan of water to the boil with salt and the vinegar

Put the lobsters in another large pan

Pour the boiling water over the lobsters off the heat

and then boil for around 9 minutes until cooked

Remove from the water and place on a tray in the fridge

When cold open the shell and carefully remove the meat

Cut into good sized pieces

FOR THE CHICKEN

3 cloves garlic, lightly crushed

7 sprigs thyme, lightly crushed

4 sprigs rosemary, lightly crushed

6 white peppercorns, lightly crushed

200kg boneless 'oyster cut' chicken thighs

Olive oil

Crush the garlic, thyme, rosemary and peppercorns

Mix with the thighs and add the olive oil to coat

Line a metal container and cook in the oven for 20 minutes at 180°C

FOR THE CHICKEN SKINS

Scrape off the excess fat from the chicken skins

Place in an oven in between 2 trays and cook at 170°C for 8 minutes or until crispy

FOR THE CURRY PASTE

4 red dried big chillies

120g chopped shallots

100g minced garlic

100g chopped Thai ginger

80g chopped lemongrass

80g Thai ginseng

50g shrimp paste

10g chopped kaffir lime peel

10g fresh or dried coriander root

10g turmeric

5g coriander seeds

5g cumin seeds

5g dry peppercorns

Add all ingredients to a blender and combine

FOR THE YELLOW CURRY

30ml oil

100g palm sugar

6 tins coconut cream

40ml fish sauce

Salt and pepper to season

Add oil, palm sugar and coconut cream to a wok on a low heat

Add yellow curry paste and bring to simmer – stir continuously for 1-2 minutes

Add coconut milk to stop burning

Add the fish sauce and season to taste and then pass through a fine sieve

FOR THE CLAWS

3 lobster claws

Dice the claw meat and place in the warm sauce

RABBIT, PISTACHIO, PICKLED CHERRIES

Serves: 8

TASTE PROFILE:

Rabbit is underused because it goes dry quickly, but by confiting it you'll keep the meat moist. Setting it into an old fashioned terrine and serving with yoghurt and pickled fruit works wonders.

Sweet:	⓪①②③④⑤
Sour:	⓪①②③④⑤⑥⑦
Bitter:	⓪①②③④⑤⑥
Salty:	⓪①②③④⑤⑥⑦
Umami:	⓪①②③④

TO CONFIT THE RABBIT

½ lemon, zest
½ orange, zest
250g rock salt
750g rabbit legs
1 clove garlic
5 sprigs thyme
2 litres duck fat
2 bay leaves

Mix zest of the citrus fruit and salt together
Lay the rabbit legs in a single layer on a tray
Completely cover with salt mixture then leave for 2 hours
Rinse cured legs clean under cold water then dry
Melt duck fat to 130°C
Add rabbit, garlic, thyme and bay leaves to the duck fat
Cover in tin foil
Cook for 2½ hours or until meat comes away from the bones
Cool the legs in the fat
Once cool, pick the meat from the bone in large pieces

TO PRESS THE CONFIT RABBIT

500g confit rabbit
100g butter
50g duck fat
30g Dijon mustard
17g table salt
Freshly ground white pepper

Bring the rabbit, duck fat and butter to room temperature and add to a bowl with the remaining ingredients
Lightly mix, don't overwork the rabbit should stay chunky
Place into container to set no deeper than 3cm
Press with cardboard then leave overnight

FOR THE PISTACHIO BISCOTTI

175g plain flour
½ tsp baking powder
1 tsp salt
175g caster sugar
100g pistachios
2 medium eggs, beaten

Sift the flour, baking powder and salt into a bowl
Add sugar, pistachio nuts and beaten eggs
Mix together with fingers then divide the mixture in half
Roll into two long sausage shapes and place on a baking tray
Bake for 20 minutes at 180°C until pale golden and just firm
Cool for 10 minutes then place in the freezer for at least an hour

For the second baking, slice as thin as possible
Place on baking tray, lined with greaseproof paper
Dry in the oven at 160°C for 8-10 minutes
Remove and cool

FOR THE PISTACHIO YOGHURT

150g pistachios
65ml pistachio oil
7g salt

Roast pistachios at 160°C for 8-10 minutes
Let cool naturally
Blend with salt in blender
Slowly add oil to form a peanut butter consistency
Pass through a fine sieve

FOR THE GREEK YOGHURT

120ml thick Greek yoghurt
70g pistachio butter
Salt

Combine the yoghurt and pistachio nuts, then season

FOR THE CHERRY PICKLE

20 cherries
100ml Amazu pickling liquid

Cut cherries in half and remove stones
Add the Amazu to the cherries and leave for 2 hours to infuse

FOR THE YUZU GEL

150g yuzu
85ml stock syrup (see basics)
4g agar
12g sugar
100ml water

Bring yuzu and stock syrup to boil
Mix agar and sugar together
When liquid is boiling, whisk in powders
Cook for 30 seconds then pour into container and rest in the fridge for 24 hours
Blend with no more the water until a mayonnaise consistency is formed

FOR THE GARNISH

Chopped toasted pistachios

TO SERVE

Ensure terrine is room temperature

OX TONGUE AND SWEETBREAD HOT POT

TASTE PROFILE:

My history in a casserole dish. I love comfort food like this and using sweet breads and ox tongue, which is my favourite offal, means it's packed with flavour. Perfect for a Sunday dinner or a rainy day.

Sweet:	0 1 2 3 4
Sour:	0 1 2 3
Bitter:	0 1 2 3
Salty:	0 1 2 3 4 5
Umami:	0 1 2 3 4 5 6

FOR THE HOT POT

500g sweetbreads

1 litre milk

100g celeriac

100g carrot

100g leeks

4 shallots, thinly sliced

4 cloves garlic, thinly sliced

1 tbsp fresh thyme, chopped

70ml Madeira wine

1 litre chicken stock

200g black pudding

Splash vegetable oil

3 large baking potatoes

Knob of butter, melted

Salt and pepper to season

Dice ox tongue into 1 inch pieces

Poach sweetbreads in milk for 3 minutes

Remove from milk and cool in fridge

Once cool, peel off skin

In a casserole dish, add a splash of vegetable oil, place on the heat

Thinly slice shallots and garlic then add to the dish

While cooking slowly, dice celeriac and carrots then set aside

Thinly slice leeks

When shallots are cooked, add leeks and chopped thyme, cook until tender

Add diced carrots, celeriac, ox tongue and sweetbreads

Mix together

Add madeira, reduce and top with chicken stock

Season with salt and pepper to taste

When it comes to the boil, remove from heat

Add black pudding and stir

Season to taste once more

Peel and thinly slice potatoes

Fan them over the top of the dish

Place into oven at 200°C for 30-35 minutes

Whilst in the oven, brush potatoes with soft butter

Season to taste and serve

OX CHEEK, CHARRED SPRING ONIONS, MASHED POTATO, ONION RINGS

Serves: 6

TASTE PROFILE:

Braised ox cheek is one of those dishes I could never say no to. The rich, sticky sauce with onion rings is a match made in heaven.

Sweet:	⓪①❷③④
Sour:	⓪①❷③④
Bitter:	⓪①②③④⑤⑥❼
Salty:	⓪①②❸④⑤
Umami:	⓪①②③④⑤❻

FOR THE OX CHEEK

3 ox cheeks
1 onion
2 carrots
4 bay leaves
5 cloves garlic
Small bunch thyme
1 litre chicken stock
1 bottle red wine
50ml soy sauce
Salt and pepper to season

Trim the ox cheeks by removing excess sinew
Peel and roughly chop the vegetables
Pan-fry ox cheeks in a large ovenproof pan, when golden brown remove from heat
Remove cheeks and put the vegetables in to fry until golden brown
Add the cheeks back into pan
Deglaze the pan with red wine and reduce by half
Add the chicken stock and herbs
Season with salt and pepper
Cover the pan with tin foil and cook in the oven for 3-4 hours at 130°C
Once cooked remove from heat and add soy sauce
Allow meat to rest in dish then when cold, remove the ox cheeks from saucepan
Pass the sauce through a sieve to remove vegetables
Season to taste
Reduce sauce by half
Add cheeks back to saucepan then place in oven to reheat

FOR THE SPRING ONIONS

Small bunch of spring onions
Butter
Salt and pepper to season

Remove outside layer from spring onions
In a smoking hot pan, scorch the spring onions
Finish with a little butter
Season with salt and pepper

FOR THE ONION RINGS

1 onion
100g cornflour
100g plain flour
200ml ice-cold sparkling water
100ml milk
50g plain flour, for dusting
Oil for deep frying
Salt for seasoning

Thinly slice the onion, keeping the rings intact
Add to the milk
In a bowl whisk the cornflour and plain flour with the sparkling water
Remove the onions from the milk
Dust in the 50g of plain flour
Dip in batter individually
Deep fry until golden brown
Remove and season with salt

FOR THE MASHED POTATO

500g of red skin potatoes, peeled
Knob of butter
Splash of milk
Salt and pepper to season

Add the potatoes to a saucepan of salted water
Simmer for 20-25 minutes until cooked
Remove from water and pass through fine sieve
Add potatoes back to pan and add knob of butter and splash of milk
Season to taste

DUCK, LAVENDER, SWEET POTATO, PEACH

TASTE PROFILE:

Roast duck has long since moved away from the traditional accompaniments of orange and cherries. Try it with something more exciting. I think roast peaches and floral lavender really bring out the flavours of the fatty, gamey meat. Fun to look at and fun to eat.

Serves: 6

Sweet: 0 1 2 3 4
Sour: 0
Bitter: 0 1 2
Salty: 0 1 2 3
Umami: 0 1 2 3 4 5 6

FOR THE DUCK

1 whole duck
1 tbsp fresh lavender
3 tbsp maple syrup
Salt

Prepare the bird for roasting by rinsing out the cavity
Slowly pan-fry the crown until golden brown and the fat has rendered down
When perfectly rendered, rub the crown in syrup, sprinkle with lavender and salt
Place the bird in an oven at 140°C for 45 minutes
Leave to rest at room temperature
When you're just about to serve the duck, put it back in the oven at 180°C for 10 minutes to get the skin really beautiful and crisp

FOR THE ROAST PEACHES

4 peaches
2 sprigs thyme
1 stick rosemary
1 bay leaf
White peppercorns
50g butter

Cut the peaches into segments
Add everything to a pan and cover
Cook on a low heat for 10 minutes, do not stir
Remove from the heat

FOR THE DUCK SAUCE

200g duck bones, chopped into 1 inch pieces
200g duck wings
300ml chicken stock
100ml white wine
100ml red wine
100g onions, finely diced
1 leek, finely sliced
100g button mushrooms
1 bouquet garni (rosemary, thyme, parsley etc...)

Roast bones and wings in the oven at 160°C until golden
Pour out the fat, reserving for the sweet potato purée
Add vegetables to the pan and caramelise
Deglaze with white and red wine, stirring to remove all the sediments
Add roasted bones and wings to a saucepan
Reduce alcohol by half
Add stock and bouquet garni
Skim continuously
Reduce by half
Pass through sieve

FOR THE SWEET POTATO PURÉE

5 sweet potatoes
70g honey
120g butter or the duck fat from the roasting bones
Salt and pepper to season

Bake the sweet potatoes in the oven on piles of salt
Once cooked, remove from heat
Pass through a drum sieve
Add to blender
Pour in honey and butter gradually and slowly blitz
Finish with seasoning

FOR THE GARNISH

Purple watercress

BONE MARROW, GIROLLES, PARSLEY, CAPERS, SOURDOUGH

TASTE PROFILE:

Sometimes, even the simplest things makes me smile. Roasted bone marrow and crispy, buttery bread will do that too.

Serves: 6

Sweet:	⓪①②③④
Sour:	⓪①②③④
Bitter:	⓪
Salty:	⓪①②③④⑤⑥
Umami:	⓪①②③④⑤⑥

FOR THE MARROW

6 beef bones, cut length ways

Roast in the oven for 7 minutes at 180°C

FOR THE PARSLEY SALAD

50g flat leaf parsley

1 tbsp baby capers

1 banana shallot

1 tbsp extra virgin olive oil

Salt and pepper to season

Pick parsley leaves from stems

Thinly slice shallot into rings

Add capers and rest of ingredients to a bowl

FOR THE SOURDOUGH

1kg Campaillou flour

20g salt

10g fresh yeast

800ml warm water

Mix all ingredients and leave to ferment for 45-60 minutes

After this time turn and dust with the flour to refresh and feed the dough

Remove from mixer and place on table for 10-15 minutes

Roll into shape

Line baking trays with baking paper

Put dough onto trays and leave for 10 minutes

Brush with water and cut to desired size

Prove until doubled in size

Brush once more with water

Place in oven at 230°C and bake for 30 minutes

FOR THE GARNISH

100g girolles

20g butter

1 clove garlic

Add butter to frying pan

When foaming, add girolles

Cook until golden

Pour over bone marrows

BEEF HEEL, BARLEY, MUSHROOMS, SORREL, SORREL PURÉE

TASTE PROFILE:

Ask your butcher for the heel of beef – it sounds bizarre because it's underused, but has a similar flavour and texture to oxtail except it doesn't have the bone. Fantastic for braising.

Sweet: ⓪①②③④
Sour: ⓪①②③④⑤
Bitter: ⓪①②③
Salty: ⓪①②③④⑤
Umami: ⓪①②③④⑤

FOR THE BEEF HEEL

2 beef heels

5 cloves garlic

1 carrot

2 onions

1 leek

4 bay leaves

2 litres chicken stock

600ml red wine

100ml white wine

Small bunch thyme

Roast the beef heel and remove from pan

Peel and roughly chop vegetables

In the roasting pan, with a little olive oil, add the vegetables and garlic and roast until golden brown

Remove vegetables from pan

Deglaze with white wine

Reduce by half

Add chicken stock and bay leaves

Add beef and vegetables back to pan

Cover with tin foil

Cook at 140°C for 3-4 hours

FOR THE BARLEY

100g barley

1 litre chicken stock

70g Parmesan

Salt and pepper to season

Soak barley in water overnight

Remove from water

Add barley to pan and add chicken stock

Simmer until barley is tender

Remove excess water

Add Parmesan

Season with salt and pepper to taste

SORREL PUREE

500g picked sorrel leaf

Salt and pepper to season

Blanche the sorrel in salted water

Refresh in ice cold water

Lightly squeeze the sorrel leaves to drain any excess water out, then blend until smooth in a blender

You may need to add a couple of ice cubes to keep the temperature down and for the liquid to blend

Finally, pass through a fine sieve and season to taste

FOR THE PICKLED MUSHROOMS

100g girolle mushrooms

100ml Amuzu pickle liquid (see basics)

Warm pickle liquid and pour over the mushrooms

Cling film the container and let sit until they go cold

GARNISH

Celeriac crumb (see basics)

Pickled dulse

Baby sorrel leaves

JERUSALEM ARTICHOKE VELOUTÉ, PANCETTA, SAGE

TASTE PROFILE:

Soups can very boring but this one made with
Jerusalem artichoke is far from it. Try it for yourself;
I've never had a bad one in my life.

Sweet:	❶❷❸	
Sour:	❶❷❸	
Bitter:	❶❷❸❹	
Salty:	❶❷❸❹❺	
Umami:	❶❷❸❹❺	

FOR THE ARTICHOKE VELOUTÉ

200g Jerusalem artichokes

100g pancetta (or smoked bacon)

250g butter

6 large shallots

6 cloves garlic

1 litre chicken stock

3 sprigs thyme

300ml cream

2 lemons

8 sage leaves

Salt and pepper for seasoning

Peel artichokes and place them into a bucket of water
with a lemon

Slice the shallots and garlic

Melt the butter and pancetta in a big saucepan with the
shallots, garlic, thyme and sage then cook slowly until
the golden brown

Slice the artichoke and add to saucepan

Add the chicken stock bringing to the boil with the
cream

When artichokes are soft, blitz until smooth

Season to taste

Finish with a squeeze of lemon

FOR THE GARNISH

Chopped chives and sage

Crispy bacon

LAMB, COURGETTE FLOWERS, GOAT'S CHEESE, HONEY

TASTE PROFILE:

This is the dish that put me into the Masterchef final, which was down to its uncomplicated approach and bags of flavour. The critics felt it was the best dish they had tasted in the programme's history. Which was nice to hear.

Serves: 6

Sweet:	⓪①②③④
Sour:	⓪①②
Bitter:	⓪①②
Salty:	⓪①②③④
Umami:	⓪①②③

FOR THE LAMB

2 lamb cannons (approximately 450g each)
50ml extra virgin olive oil
3 sprigs thyme
1 sprig rosemary
3 bay leaves

Remove top layer of sinew from the lamb
Place the lamb, fat side down, in a cold frying pan with the olive oil
Roast the lamb to render away the fat and then drain the excess fat away
Add the herbs and turn the lamb
Cook at 120°C for 9 minutes
Leave to rest slightly before cutting

FOR THE WHOLE COURGETTES WITH FLOWERS

5 shallots, finely diced
50ml olive oil
8 sprigs thyme, chopped
50ml honey
500g goat's cheese
6 courgette flowers
Salt and pepper to season
Plain flour for dusting
Oil for deep frying

Finely dice shallots
Cook shallots until roasted in a saucepan with the olive oil and chopped thyme
Season to taste
Allow to cool
Add the honey and goat's cheese and beat with a spoon
Spoon the goat's cheese into the flowers
Lightly flour then deep fry until crispy

FOR THE COURGETTE AND BASIL PURÉE

5 courgettes
1 bunch basil
50ml olive oil
5 cloves garlic

Peel the courgettes, discarding the flesh but keeping the peel
Finely chop the peel, pick the basil leaves
Add olive oil to a large saucepan with the garlic and courgette peel
Cook until golden brown, add the basil, and blend

FOR THE GARNISH

Quenelles of goat's cheese mixture

162

DESSERTS

Being brought up surrounded by the smell of baking at home, it was inevitable that I would love pastry that remains my passion.

Like the rest of my cooking my desserts have simple ingredients but are big on flavour.

The most important thing when making a dessert is precision. You must weigh everything out accurately or the end product will be a disappointment.

Remember each recipe has only five or six ingredients so don't be lazy, weigh everything as instructed. Precision makes the execution perfect.

I love desserts so much that I recently introduced my own range of chocolate; the Adam Handling Classic in dark, milk and white and also the Adam Handling Retro range containing some nice surprising flavours. Made from blends devised by myself and my chocolatier, they are available from my website www.adamhandling.co.uk and quality outlets.

SALTED CARAMEL PARFAIT, CHOCOLATE, PASSION FRUIT

TASTE PROFILE:

This dish is a little more complicated as it's the dessert I made when I won British Chef of the Year. The different types of chocolate alongside the salted caramel parfait and acidic passion fruit creates a dish full of contrasting flavours and textures.

Serves: 8

Sweet: ⓿①②③④⑤⑥⑦⑧
Sour: ⓿①②③④⑤⑥⑦⑧⑨
Bitter: ⓿①②③
Salty: ⓿①②
Umami: ⓿

FOR THE CARAMEL PARFAIT

60g hazelnuts

280g caster sugar

6 large egg whites

400ml double cream

Place nuts on a tray and toast in the oven for 3-4 minutes

Heat a saucepan on the stove and pour in 120g of the sugar and caramelise

Add the warm nuts and stir together

Pour the caramelised nuts on to a silicone mat or greaseproof tray and allow to cool

When at room temperature and set, smash into little pieces to make praline

In a clean bowl whisk the egg whites to a soft peak

Add the remaining sugar and beat to a stiff peak

Fold the chopped praline into the meringue

Whisk the cream to soft peaks

Fold into the meringue mixture

Pipe into moulds then freeze until set

Remove from moulds and keep in the freezer

FOR THE WHITE SPRAY

200g cocoa butter

200g white chocolate

Melt both together and add to a spray gun

Spray with 1 coat then place in the freezer for 10 minutes – repeat this 3 times

FOR THE PASSION FRUIT SORBET

1 litre passion fruit coulis

200g nappage (see basics)

Mix both together and place in the freezer

When frozen add to a blender and blend until smooth

Place back in the freezer to set

FOR THE CHOCOLATE AERO

900g chocolate, melted and tempered

100ml olive oil

Temper the chocolate and mix with the olive oil

Place mix in a siphon gun and charge 3 times

Shake siphon to agitate mixture

Leave for 5 minutes in gun at room temperature

Pipe into moulds and leave to set at room temperature

Store at room temperature in airtight container

FOR THE CHOCOLATE SPONGE

104g egg white

100g 70% cocoa chocolate, melted

67g egg yolks

67g sugar

17g flour

Place all ingredients except the egg whites in blender and blend for 5 minutes

Whisk the egg white to a soft peak

Mix all together

Line a small deep cake tin

Cook in the oven at 200°C for 7-8 minutes

Let set and cool down

Rip with your hands when needed

STRAWBERRY AND WATERMELON

TASTE PROFILE:

Strawberries are a wonderful berry when picked at the right time of year, in the Summer. This is such an uncomplicated dessert with fresh, dried and frozen strawberries all blending together sumptuously.

Serves: 8

Sweet:	⓪①❷❸❹❺❻❼
Sour:	⓪①❷❸❹
Bitter:	⓪①❷❸
Salty:	⓪
Umami:	⓪

FOR THE COMPRESSED WATERMELON

200g watermelon

200ml strawberry syrup

Dice watermelon into 1 inch squares and place 9 squares into small container

Add some strawberry syrup to each container

FOR THE STRAWBERRY JUICE

800g strawberries

200g sugar

2 lemons, juice

Blend all the ingredients in a blender

Pass through sieve

FOR THE STRAWBERRY TUILE

100g strawberry purée

54g sugar

15g glucose

Bring all the ingredients to boil

Spread thinly on a tray

Dry in the oven

FOR THE YOGHURT JELLY

330g Greek yoghurt

70ml stock syrup (see basics)

½ vanilla pod, seeds only

2 gelatine leaves

Boil syrup and add the gelatine

Add the vanilla seeds to the yoghurt then pour the warm syrup mixture over the yoghurt and mix thoroughly

Pour mixture into lined container and set in fridge

Once set cut into 2cm squares and place back in fridge prior to serving

FOR THE STRAWBERRY SORBET

1 litre strawberry purée

50g whole milk

245g sugar

50g glucose

Boil all ingredients together

Freeze mix once cool

Blend until smooth

FOR THE STRAWBERRY MOUSSE

400ml strawberry purée

3 egg yolks

125g sugar

5 gelatine leaves

400g semi-whipped cream

Boil strawberry purée

Sabayon the egg yolks and sugar and pour over the strawberry purée

Add the gelatine to the mix and cool

Once cooled, fold in the semi-whipped cream and place in fridge to set

To serve whip mixture and either pipe onto the plate, or place in quenelles

CHOCOLATE, CHERRIES AND HAZELNUTS

TASTE PROFILE:

This is a delicious dessert for chocolate lovers, with a stand out cherry flavour and my famous burnt butter cake.

Sweet:	⓿❶❷❸❹❺
Sour:	⓿❶❷❸❹❺❻
Bitter:	⓿❶❷❸❹❺❻
Salty:	⓿❶❷
Umami:	⓿

FOR THE CHERRY MARSHMALLOW

225g sugar
60g glucose
75ml water
17g powdered gelatine
100ml cherry purée
Icing sugar for dusting

Place cherry purée into mixer
Bring sugar, glucose and water to 121°C
Add gelatine to syrup and pour onto cherry purée and whisk on high speed until mix is light and fluffy
Line a tray with greaseproof paper and grease spray
Pour mix on to tray and smooth out
Leave to set in fridge for 1 hour
Cut marshmallow into ½ inch squares, powder with icing sugar before serving

FOR THE KIRSCH ICE CREAM

300ml semi-skimmed milk
600ml double cream
500g sugar
225g egg yolk
75ml kirsch

Boil cream and milk
Whisk egg yolk and sugar and pour over milk and cream
Bring mix to 82°C and remove from stove
Add kirsch to mix
Pour into an ice cream maker and churn

FOR THE DEHYDRATED AERO

125g 72%+ cocoa chocolate
2 egg yolks
5 egg whites
45g sugar

Melt chocolate, set aside
Sabayon egg yolks and fold into chocolate
Whip egg whites and sugar and fold into chocolate mix
Spread about ½ inch thick on to silicone mat or greaseproof paper and slowly dry at 90°C for 12 hours
Snap into shards for service

FOR THE MILK CHOCOLATE GANACHE

800g milk chocolate
350g cream

Melt chocolate in microwave
Boil cream and allow to cool slightly
Fold the cooled cream into the chocolate in thirds, until fully emulsified

FOR THE HAZELNUT & BURNT BUTTER CAKE

230g plain flour
11g baking powder
5g Maldon salt
3 eggs
400g dark brown sugar
250ml whole milk
120g brown butter
140g hazelnut praline
50g salted peanuts, toasted and lightly crushed

Preheat the oven to 150°C
Spray a small cake tin with non-stick spray
In a small bowl sieve together flour and baking powder then add the salt
In a large bowl whisk the eggs, brown sugar, milk, brown butter and praline
Using a rubber spatula, fold the flour mixture and toasted nuts into the egg mixture
Transfer the batter to the a lined baking tray, spreading evenly
Bake for 75 minutes or until spongy
Let cool in the pan or on a wire rack
When serving, lightly tear the cake in to small pieces

LEMON TART

TASTE PROFILE:

My take on the classic tarte au citron; fresh lemon with sweet raspberries and crispy meringues. A great little dessert.

Serves: 8

Sweet: ⓿❶❷❸❹
Sour: ⓿❶❷❸❹❺❻❼❽
Bitter: ⓿❶❷❸
Salty: ⓿
Umami: ⓿

FOR THE LEMON TART MIX

5 eggs
310g sugar
250g lemon juice
310g double cream

Whisk eggs and sugar
Boil cream and pour slowly over egg mix
Add lemon juice to mix and place in fridge overnight
Remove from fridge and discard froth layer from the mix
Set aside until tart case is ready

FOR THE SWEET PASTE

625g flour
250g icing sugar
250g butter
2 eggs
1 egg yolk

Combine the flour, sugar and butter to form a crumb
Once butter is incorporated, add eggs and form a dough
Allow to rest in fridge for at least 2 hours
Roll out dough and line a small greaseproof baking tray with sweet paste and blind bake at 180°C
Once shell is made, brush with egg yolk
Pour lemon tart mix into tart case and bake at 130°C for 20 minutes or until mix is just set in the middle
Remove from oven and cool at room temperature
Place in fridge for a further 1 hour and cut into 12cm by 3cm rectangle
Reserve in fridge until needed

FOR THE MERINGUE

250g sugar
60g water
5 egg whites

Whip egg whites to soft peaks using an electric whisk
In a saucepan bring sugar and water to 119°C, pour over egg whites and whip until cool
Place meringue into piping bags and pipe peaks onto lemon tart before serving

FOR THE RASPBERRY JELLY

800g raspberries
200g sugar
2 lemons, juiced
3g agar

Blitz and pass raspberries through sieve until you have 200ml of juice
Add the sugar, lemon juice and agar to the juice and boil
Pour a thick layer onto a metal tray and set in fridge
Once set, cut out 12cm by 3cm rectangles and place in container until needed
Place raspberry strip on lemon tart and pipe on meringue

FOR THE CONFIT LEMON

1 lemon, zest only no pith
100ml water
100g sugar

Zest lemon using peeler and cut into thin strips
Place zest into saucepan and boil until a small amount of water remains
Repeat this process 4 times, the last time add the sugar and reduce to a thin syrup
Pour zest with syrup into container and place in fridge

FOR THE RASPBERRY SORBET

1 litre raspberry purée
100g nappage (see basics)
½ lemon, juiced

Add all ingredients together, blend for 1 minute then pass through a fine sieve and freeze overnight
After frozen solid, blend again until smooth
Add back to the freezer and leave for 30 minutes to set

FOR THE RASPBERRY MERINGUE

250g sugar
60g water
5 egg whites, whipped
1 punnet fresh whole raspberries

Whip the egg whites
Bring sugar and water to 119°C in saucepan
Pour over egg whites and whip until cool
Spread mix onto a silicone mat or greaseproof paper and dry in a low oven until crisp
Break down meringue into shards and place in container

CHOCOLATE AND MANDARIN CHEESECAKE

Serves: 8

TASTE PROFILE:

A funky way of doing a cheescake or a flourless chocolate cake using dried mandarins. Perfect with a cup of tea or after a big meal.

Sweet: ⓿❶❷❸❹❺❻
Sour: ⓿❶❷❸
Bitter: ⓿❶❷
Salty: ⓿
Umami: ⓿

FOR THE FLOURLESS CHOCOLATE CAKE

100g 70% cocoa dark chocolate

100g butter

100g icing sugar

100g egg white

100g ground almonds

Melt butter and chocolate together

In mixer combine the icing sugar and ground almonds, add the melted butter and chocolate and continue to mix

Once mixed slowly add the egg whites and mix on the slowest speed

Half fill the moulds with the mixture

Bake at 165°C for 8 minutes or until cooked

Allow to cool and cut into 12cm by 3cm fingers

FOR THE MANDARIN CHEESECAKE

500g cream cheese

175g sugar

3 mandarins, zested

25ml cream

3 gelatine leaves

400ml semi-whipped cream

Beat cream cheese, sugar and mandarin zest in mixer

Boil 25ml of cream and add gelatine leaves

Pour the gelatine mix into cream cheese mix and combine

Remove from mixer and fold in the semi whipped cream

Place mix in fridge to set

Once set place cheesecake mix into piping bag with a large round nozzle and pipe cheesecake along the cake finger

TO GARNISH

Finish with fresh mandarin segments along the cheesecake and add some chocolate curls

POPCORN, SALTED CARAMEL, CHOCOLATE SORBET

TASTE PROFILE:

Salted caramel and chocolate is a fashionable flavour combination – adding the toasted popcorn mousse and crisp sugar cylinders is not only different but incredibly tasty.

Serves: 8

Sweet: ⓪①②③④
Sour: ⓪①②
Bitter: ⓪①②③④⑤
Salty: ⓪①②③④
Umami: ⓪

FOR THE CROQUANT TUBES

140g sugar
30ml water
100g glucose

Add everything to a saucepan and melt to make a caramel
When golden brown pour the caramel on a sugar mat or greaseproof baking tray and leave to cool
Break-up and blitz in a blender to make a sugar powder
Using square stencil, dust on a large amount of the sugar powder on to a silicone mat or baking tray and cook in the oven at 180°C for 3 minutes
Roll the sugar squares around wooden roller to make tubes

FOR THE POPCORN MOUSSE

100g popcorn kernels, popped
200ml milk
200ml cream
3 yolks
100g sugar
5 gelatine leaves
300ml double cream

Soak gelatine in ice-cold water to go pliable
Boil milk and cream, remove from heat then add the popcorn, leave to infuse for 30 minutes
Whisk yolks and sugar together until it goes white and thick
Sieve the milk and bring back to a boil then pour over the beaten egg yolks
Cook out to a custard and add the gelatine
Sieve then cool the custard in a fridge but do not set
Semi-whip cream and fold into cooled crème anglaise
Put mix in fridge then into piping bags

FOR THE SALTED CARAMEL

500g sugar
50ml water
25g glucose
4g Maldon salt
300ml cream
175g butter

Add the water, sugar, glucose and salt to a saucepan and heat until it makes a dark caramel
Once caramelised add butter and whisk
When all butter has melted add cream slowly and reboil
Pass mix through sieve and blitz using hand blender and put in fridge overnight
Place in piping bags

FOR THE NUTELLA POWDER

120g Nutella
80g tapioca flour

Place ingredients into a blender and mix
Pulse blender, shake and repeat process 6 times until fluffy
Place in airtight container at room temperature

FOR THE CARAMEL POPCORN

30g popcorn kernels, popped
100g dark brown sugar
20ml water
50g butter

Make caramel from water and sugar
Add butter and toss popcorn through to coat in caramel
Place on greaseproof paper to cool
Place in container at room temperature

FOR THE CHOCOLATE SORBET

300g 72%+ cocoa chocolate, chunks
500ml water
60g glucose

Boil glucose and water
Cool for 5 minutes and pour over chocolate chunks while whisking
Place mixture in blender and blitz for 3 minutes
Place mix in a container and freeze

FOR THE NOUGAT

175g sugar
50ml water
50g glucose
20g honey
1 egg white
10g popcorn kernels, popped
100g peanuts

Heat sugar and water to 119°C
Add honey and glucose to syrup and reboil
Whip egg white in mixer and slowly pour syrup over
Whip until cooled but still slightly warm to touch
Remove from mixer and mix with peanuts and popcorn
Place into cling film lined tray that has been sprayed with bake spray then dry overnight
Cut into squares

RHUBARB AND APPLE

TASTE PROFILE:
Rhubarb and apple is pure British heritage; we all love it, it's tried and tested and is something I really enjoy to eat.

Serves: 8

Sweet:	0 1 2 3
Sour:	0 1 2 3 4 5 6 7 8 9
Bitter:	0 1 2 3 4
Salty:	0
Umami:	0

FOR THE POACHED RHUBARB

8 sticks rhubarb
Grenadine to cover

Peel rhubarb and cut into 9cm batons
Place rhubarb and the grenadine into a ovenproof dish and leave for 1 hour
Place in the oven at 100°C for 20 minutes

FOR THE APPLE CHERVIL SAUCE

4 Granny Smith apples
Bunch chervil
60g water
Lemon, juiced
10g tapioca flour

Place all ingredients into blender and blitz for 3 minutes
Pass through fine sieve
Add the tapioca flour and whisk thoroughly
Finish with a squeeze of lemon

FOR THE POACHED APPLE

1 Granny Smith apples
Apple juice

Peel and ball the apples with a melon baller and add enough apple juice to poach the apple balls
Gently heat in small saucepan 5 minutes then leave to infuse for 2 hours

FOR THE APPLE SORBET

8 Granny Smith apples
200g sugar
400ml water
100g glucose
300g nappage (see basics)

Cut and freeze apples including skin
Boil all other ingredients and chill
Once apples are frozen add to blender with cooled syrup and blitz for 3 minutes
Put mix into containers and freeze

FOR THE YOGHURT

340g yoghurt
227g cream
32g sugar
1 gelatine leaf

Soften the gelatine in cold water
Heat half the cream in a saucepan and add gelatine
Blend all of the other ingredients in the blender and add the cream mixture
Leave to set in the fridge

FOR THE RHUBARB SYRUP

Use excess liquid from poached rhubarb and reduce by half in a saucepan on a medium heat to make a syrup

FOR THE MUSCOVADO TUILE

140g sugar
30ml water
100g glucose
50g muscovado sugar

Bring all ingredients except muscavado to a light caramel
Once done add muscavado and stir gently
Pour mix on to greaseproof paper and leave to cool and harden
Once hardened blitz in blender to a powder
Using a stencil and a tea sieve, sprinkle mix onto silicone mat or greaseproof paper to create triangles
Place mix in oven at 180°C for about 2 minutes until sugar has melted
Once translucent remove from oven and allow to cool slightly
Once mix is still pliable to the hand, shape into curls
Leave to go hard and place in airtight container

CHOCOLATE AND BLACKBERRIES

TASTE PROFILE:
These truffles have been designed with my chocolate brand Adam Handling Classic Range in mind.
The balance of chocolate and acidic blackberries works perfectly.

Serves: 8

Sweet: ⓪①②❸④⑤
Sour: ⓪①②❸④⑤
Bitter: ⓪①②③④❺⑥
Salty: ⓪❶②③④
Umami: ⓪

CHOCOLATE SHORTBREAD

200g butter
90g icing sugar
50g cocoa powder
200g flour

Beat butter and icing sugar together till fluffy
Add the flour and cocoa powder and mix
Roll mix between two sheets of greaseproof paper to abour 3cm thickness and set in fridge
Cut shortbread into rectangles and cook at 180°C for 8 minutes
Allow to cool and break into shards

BLACKBERRY GEL

400g blackberries
200g sugar
2 lemon juice

Blend the blackberries and heat all the ingredients in a small saucepan, reduce slowly to make a gel then pass through a sieve to remove the seeds

CHOCOLATE TRUFFLES

450g 64% cocoa dark chocolate
300ml single cream
4 yolks
50g sugar
450ml double cream

Boil the 300ml cream and pour over chocolate
Mix until fully incorporated to make a ganache
Whisk the sugar and egg yolks until white and fluffy
Fold egg mix into cooled ganache
Semi-whip 450ml cream and fold into chocolate mix
Pipe mixture into small metal ring moulds and freeze
Using a small cutter cut the centre out
Using chocolate glaze cover truffles while still frozen and place in fridge until needed
When glazed place on the shortbread and fill the centre with the blackberry gel

CHOCOLATE GLAZE

75ml water
180ml sugar
150ml cream
65g glucose
4 gelatine leaves
60g cocoa powder

Boil the water, sugar, cream and glucose together
Soften gelatine in a little water and add to boiled syrup
Add cocoa powder and blend with hand blender till smooth and place in fridge until needed
When reheating warm between 36-40°C so as not to melt the truffles when coating

BLACKBERRY ICE CREAM

1 pint milk
750ml cream
115g egg yolks
250g sugar
50g fresh blackberries

In a saucepan add the milk and cream and boil
In another saucepan, combine the egg yolks and sugar and whisk until pale and fluffy
Off the heat, pour the hot milk and cream over the egg yolks and stir to make a custard
Put the liquid back on the heat and cook slowly until thickened
Blitz the blackberries and sieve out the pips
Add to the custard mixture
Chill mix in fridge then put into ice cream machine

PEAR AND ELDERFLOWER

TASTE PROFILE:

You may have seen this dish from my guest mentor appearance on the amateur Masterchef – since it was screened I have had so many people asking me for the recipe – so I decided to put it in my book. Very simple, clean on flavour and positively delicious.

Serves: 8

Sweet:	0 1 2 3 4
Sour:	0 1 2 3 4
Bitter:	0 1 2
Salty:	0
Umami:	0

POACHED PEARS AND CARAMEL SYRUP

8 pears

165ml water

150g sugar

Peel and quarter the pears, and remove the pips and stem

Make a caramel by heating 15ml water with the sugar then add the rest of water and heat to make a syrup

Pour this syrup over the pears

Roast the pears in the oven for about 20 minutes on 160°C depending on the ripeness of the pears

MERINGUE SHEETS

100g egg white

200g sugar

10g lemon juice

10g raspberry powder

Whip egg white and slowly add sugar till all added

Add lemon juice and whip for a further 1 minute

Spread this onto the silicone mat or greaseproof paper and sprinkle over powder

Place in the oven at 100°C for 1 hour until crisp

MARSHMALLOW

225g sugar

60g glucose

75g water

17g gelatine powder

100g raspberry purée

Bring sugar, water and glucose to 119°C in saucepan, and add the gelatine powder

Add purée to mixing bowl with whisk attachment; slowly add syrup to purée while whisking until the mixture is fully aerated

Line a tray with cling film and spray with a little oil to stop marshmallows from sticking. Place on rack until set then cut into cubes

ELDERFLOWER PANNA COTTA

300g milk

300g cream

60g sugar

3 gelatine leaves

20ml elderflower cordial

Soften the gelatine in some water

Meanwhile the milk, cream and sugar then add the softened gelatine

Add cordial at end and mix. Place in a container and seal with cling film to avoid a skin forming

Cool slightly before pouring into bowls

ROAST HAZELNUTS

100g hazelnuts, blanched

Place blanched hazelnuts on tray and coat in olive oil, add a pinch of salt and sugar and mix in

Roast at 180°C for about 6 minutes until golden brown

MARINATED SUMMER BERRIES WITH ELDERFLOWER SORBET

TASTE PROFILE:

British berries are by far some of the best in the world, and marinating them in a strawberry soup with refreshing elderflower sorbet is perfect for any Summer's night.

Serves: 6

Sweet:	⓪①②❸❹❺
Sour:	⓪①②❸❹❺
Bitter:	⓪❶❷❸
Salty:	⓪
Umami:	⓪

FOR THE BERRIES

300g strawberries

100g blueberries

100g raspberries

50g red currants

50g gooseberries

Handful baby mint, chopped

Handful baby lemon balm, chopped

Icing sugar

Prepare by removing stalks and cutting all the berries into small equal pieces

Combine all the berries together with the chopped mint and lemon balm leaves

If the berries are slightly sour, mix in a little icing sugar

FOR THE FRUIT SOUP

200g strawberries

50g caster sugar

50g Armagnac

100g Port

Remove the stalks and cut the strawberries into quarters

Add strawberries with the sugar to a small saucepan

Place on a low heat and cook until tender

Add the Armagnac and Port

Cook for 5 minutes then pass through a fine sieve

ELDERFLOWER SORBET

500ml milk

140ml cream

40g glucose

130g caster sugar

40g milk powder

6g gelatine powder

200ml elderflower cordial

Warm cream, milk and glucose

Add the sugar and milk powder and bring to the boil

Remove the milk mixture from the heat and add gelatine

Mix to dissolve

Pass through a sieve

Add elderflower cordial

Place in a container and freeze

When frozen solid add to a blender and blend until smooth to break up the ice crystals

Refreeze to harden

LIME PARFAIT, MINT, MANGO, PINEAPPLE

TASTE PROFILE:

A modern way to present this dish – frozen lime parfait with the different types of mango makes for some amazing flavours and textures. This one will definitely get people talking at a dinner party.

Serves: 8

Sweet: ⓪①②③④⑤
Sour: ⓪①②③④⑤⑥⑦
Bitter: ⓪①②
Salty: ⓪
Umami: ⓪

FOR THE MANGO PURÉE

5 mangos, puréed

50ml stock syrup (see basics)

½ lime, zested

2 gelatine leaves

Boil syrup and lime zest and add the gelatine

Strain over the mango purée, place in a blender and blitz for 2 minutes

Place in fridge to set for 1 hour

FOR THE FRESH MANGO DISCS

1 mango, peeled

Slice mango into thin strips and cut out rings using cutter

FOR THE CARAMELISED PINEAPPLE

150g small diced pineapple

50g sugar

Freshly ground black pepper

Make a dry caramel by melting the sugar over a high-heat in a saucepan – try not to stir too often

Quickly add pineapple and caramelise

Remove from heat and sprinkle with fresh black pepper

FOR THE YOGHURT JELLY

330g Greek yoghurt

70ml stock syrup (see basics)

½ vanilla pod, seeds only

2 gelatine leaves

Boil syrup and add the gelatine

Add the vanilla seeds to the yoghurt then pour the warm syrup mixture over the yoghurt and mix thoroughly

Pour mixture into lined container and set in fridge

Once set cut into 2cm squares and place back in fridge prior to serving

FOR THE LIME PARFAIT

6 egg yolks

140g sugar

30g water

400g double cream, lightly whipped

2 limes, zested

Sabayon egg yolks in an electric mixer by whipping until white

Bring sugar and water to 119°C

Pour over egg yolks and whisk until cooled slightly

Add lime zest to sabayon when still warm and whisk

Once cooled, fold in lightly whipped cream and set mix in lined cones made from greaseproof paper

Place cones in a freezer for a few hours until set and frozen

PEACH, PISTACHIO, WHITE CHOCOLATE

Serves: 8

TASTE PROFILE:

A simple peach dessert with a punchy pistachio flourless cake, an invigorating peach sorbet and poppy seeds for texture. A very light and refreshing dish.

Sweet:	0 1 2 3 4
Sour:	0 1 2 3 4 5
Bitter:	0 1 2
Salty:	0
Umami:	0

FOR THE PEACH

4 peaches

25ml elderflower juice

60g sugar

1 lime, zested

Chinese Schezuan pepper, ground

Segment the peaches into eighths then gently peel off the skin

Infuse the elderflower with sugar, lime and pepper on a low heat for 5 minutes

Add the peach segments then turn off the heat and allow to slowly poach

FOR THE PISTACHIO CAKE

64g ground almonds

104g skinned pistachios

126g unsalted butter

96g icing sugar

12g pistachio paste

4 large eggs

Grease a baking tray and line with paper

Blend the ground almonds and pistachio nuts together, until fine

In an electric mixer combine the butter, icing sugar, ground nuts and pistachio paste

Mix until smooth then add the eggs one by one and continue to mix until a batter is formed

Pour the batter into a lined baking tray or cake tin

Place in the oven for 17-20 minutes

Remove from the oven and allow to cool on the tray or a wire rack

FOR THE PEACH SORBET

½ litre peach purée

125g nappage (see basics)

Blend all ingredients together in a blender

Freeze in a container until solid

Blend again until smooth

Freeze again to set

FOR THE MERINGUES

3 egg whites

120g sugar

Freshly ground black pepper

78ml water

Whip the egg whites

Boil sugar and water to 121°C

Pour this over the egg whites

Pipe on to a baking tray and sprinkle with pepper

Cook at 100°C for 2 hours

TO GARNISH

White chocolate of your choice

Fresh peach, thinly sliced

RASPBERRY AND ELDERFLOWER TRIFLE

TASTE PROFILE:

I used to love eating trifles as a child as a Sunday treat and I've never stopped loving them - which is why there's one in my book!

Sweet: ⓿❶❷❸❹❺❻
Sour: ⓿❶❷❸❹
Bitter: ⓿
Salty: ⓿
Umami: ⓿

FOR THE SPONGE

4 eggs
125g sugar
125g plain flour

Sabayon eggs and sugar to high peaks

Carefully fold in flour, mixing a little at a time

Spread mix onto lined tray and cook at 180°C for about 8 minutes or until slightly coloured and cooked

Allow to cool and cut out small discs small enough to fit into bottom of the shot glass

FOR THE RASPBERRY JELLY

800g raspberries
200g sugar
2 lemons, juiced
3 gelatine leaves

Blend all the ingredients, except the gelatine, in a blender but reserve a few whole raspberries

Pass through a sieve

Bring to the boil and dissolve the gelatine

Pour the mix into shot glasses with a few of the reserved whole raspberries and set in the fridge

FOR THE ELDERFLOWER JELLY

320g elderflower cordial
150g water
1 lemon, juice

Boil all the ingredients in a saucepan and pour thin layer on top of raspberry jelly

FOR THE CRÈME PATISSIERE

1 litre milk
1 vanilla pod, split
180g egg yolks
50g cornflour
250g sugar
50g plain flour

Mix the sugar, flour, cornflour, egg yolks in a bowl and whisk

Boil milk and vanilla pod then pour over the egg yolks

Pour back in the saucepan and cook until thickened and whisk until cool

Pipe the custard on top of the jelly

CHANTILLY CREAM

200g double cream
20g icing sugar
½ vanilla pod, seeds

Combine the cream, icing sugar and seeds from vanilla pod, whip then place into piping bag with star nozzle and pipe into glasses atop your custard

Finish off the trifles with some violas and fresh raspberries

RASPBERRY MARSHMALLOW FONDANT

TASTE PROFILE:

Everyone loves a chocolate fondant, and adding a flavoured marshmallow in the centre takes it to a whole new level. Any kid or adult would absolutely love this dish.

Serves: 8

Sweet: ❶❷❸❹❺❻
Sour: ❶
Bitter: ❶❷❸❹
Salty: ❶❷
Umami: ❶

FOR THE CAKE

135g 64%+ cocoa chocolate

135g butter

5 large eggs

180g sugar

70g plain flour

25g cocoa powder

5g salt

8 Raspberry marshmallows

Melt the chocolate and butter together in a microwave or saucepan

Whisk the eggs and sugar together until pale and fluffy

Gently fold in the melted chocolate mixture

Sieve the flour and cocoa powder together and fold into the chocolate mixture

Add the salt

Place the mixture into a piping bag and chill for 1 hour

Line 8 6cm diameter ring moulds with silicone paper or greaseproof paper

Half fill each ring mould with the fondant mixture

Place a large marshmallow into the centre of each fondant

Encase the marshmallow completely with the remaining fondant mixture

Leave at least a 2cm gap at the top of the ring

Refrigerate until needed

Cook at 160°C for 9 minutes

FOR THE RASPBERRY MARSHMALLOW

225g sugar

60g glucose

75g water

17g gelatine powder

100g raspberry purée

Bring sugar, water and glucose to 119°C in saucepan, and add the gelatine powder

Add purée to mixing bowl with whisk attachment; slowly add syrup to purée while whisking until the mixture is fully aerated

Line a tray with cling film and spray with a little oil to stop marshmallows from sticking. Place on rack until set then cut into cubes

HAZELNUT AND BURNT BUTTER CAKE

TASTE PROFILE:

My burnt butter cake made its debut on Masterchef:
The Professionals and had a massive response, so it's
only right I share the recipe in my book.

Sweet: ➊➋➌➍➎➏
Sour: ⓪
Bitter: ❶❷
Salty: ❶❷❸❹
Umami: ⓪

FOR THE CAKE

100g plain flour

130g whole wheat flour

11g baking powder

5g Maldon salt

3 large eggs

400g dark brown sugar

250ml whole milk

120g brown butter

140g hazelnut praline

50g salted peanuts nuts, toasted and lightly crushed

Preheat the oven to 150°C

Spray a small baking tray with non-stick spray

In a small bowl sieve together both flours and baking
powder

Add the salt

In a large bowl whisk the eggs, brown sugar, milk, brown
butter and praline

Using a rubber spatula, fold the flour mixture and toasted
nuts into the egg mixture

Transfer the batter to the lined tray, spreading evenly

Bake for 1 hour 15 minutes or until spongy

Let cool in pan on a wire rack

PISTACHIO CAKE

TASTE PROFILE:

Michel Roux Jr. told me this was one of the best cakes he'd ever eaten. It's light and packed full of pistachio flavour.

Serves: 8

Sweet: ⓪①❷③④⑤❻
Sour: ⓪
Bitter: ⓪
Salty: ⓪❶②❸❹
Umami: ⓪

FOR THE CAKE

100g ground almonds

150g pistachio nuts, skinned

170g unsalted butter, softened

125g icing sugar

21g pistachio paste

5 large eggs

Grease a baking tray and line with paper

Blend the ground almonds and pistachio nuts together, until fine

In the bowl of an electric mixer, attach the paddle and combine the butter, icing sugar, ground nuts and pistachio paste

Mix until smooth, adding the eggs one by one

Preheat the oven to 165°C

Pour the batter into the lined tray

Place in the oven for 17-20 minutes

Remove from the oven and allow to cool on the tray

CHOCOLATE ORANGE TORTE

TASTE PROFILE:

This cake is all about chocolate and orange;
the fantastic chocolate with rock salt really
counterbalances the flavour of the orange.

Sweet: 0 1 2 3 4 5
Sour: 0
Bitter: 0 1 2 3 4
Salty: 0 1 2 3 4
Umami: 0 1 2 3

FOR THE BASE

200g butter
90g icing sugar
50g cocoa powder
200g flour

Beat butter and icing sugar together till fluffy

Add the flour and cocoa powder and mix

Roll mix between two sheets of greaseproof paper to
abour 3cm thickness and set in fridge

Cut shortbread into rectangles and cook at 180°C for
8 minutes

FOR THE TORTE

375g 72%+ cocoa chocolate

2 gelatine leaves

150g glucose

900g double cream

2g salt

50g water

25ml orange oil

Soak the gelatine in iced water until pliable

In a medium saucepan bring the water and glucose to
the boil

Separately, bring the cream to the boil and combine with
the other liquid

Pour hot cream mix over chocolate

Mix until completely combined

Add salt and orange oil

Mix thoroughly and pour into lined moulds

NEVER-FAIL RASPBERRY SOUFFLÉ

TASTE PROFILE:

This 'never fail' soufflé should do just that, never fail. It's not a traditional soufflé – I call it marshmallow as it's more fluffy and light compared to the classic eggy-dense soufflé.

Serves: 8

Sweet: ⓪①②③④⑤⑥⑦⑧
Sour: ⓪①②③④
Bitter: ⓪
Salty: ⓪
Umami: ⓪

FOR THE RASPBERRY PURÉE

400g fresh raspberries

60g sugar

6g cornflour

50ml water

Blend raspberries to a purée

Pass through a sieve to remove seeds

Place purée in a saucepan and bring to the boil

In a separate saucepan, add the sugar and 25ml of the water and bring to a boil, cook until sugar starts to change to a light brown colour

When the sugar has changed colour, pour into the just-boiled purée

Mix the cornflour with remaining 25ml of water and add to the saucepan then whisk until fully incorporated

Place in a bowl and cover with cling film and allow to cool until needed

FOR THE SOUFFLÉ

6 egg whites

200g sugar

Knob of butter

Butter ramekins, then coat with some sugar, shaking out any excess

Place ramekins in a freezer

In another bowl whisk the egg whites, make sure this is grease free or they will not stiffen

When they have started to form, sprinkle over half of the sugar and whisk again

Just before the whites are at stiff peak, sprinkle over the rest of the sugar

Stop whisking when whites are shiny

Take one third of the whites and beat into the cold raspberry base making a smooth paste

With a spatula, gently fold the remaining egg whites, until completely folded into the base

Spoon the mix on to the top of the pot

Tip the soufflé mix in to the ramekins and tap them to release air bubbles

Using a palette knife scrape the excess off the top of the pot

Wipe butter around the inside of the pot to ensure the soufflé doesn't stick and dust with sugar

Place the ramekins on a tray and bake in the oven for 7-8 minutes at 180°C

Remove from the oven and dust with icing sugar

THE BASICS

FOCACCIA

Serves: 8

TASTE PROFILE:

Focaccia is definitely one of the most flavoursome breads; roast garlic, rosemary and sunblushed tomatoes are my choice of ingredients but play around and add your own to put your stamp on it.

Sweet:　⓪①②❸❹❺
Sour:　⓪①❷❸
Bitter:　⓪①❷❸❹
Salty:　⓪①②❸❹❺
Umami:　⓪①❷❸❹

TO MAKE THE FOCACCIA

400g T55 bread flour

250ml water

50ml olive oil

20g yeast

8g salt

Pinch of sugar

Whole garlic cloves

Sun blushed tomatoes

Fresh rosemary

Warm up water then add yeast and a pinch of sugar

Leave to sit for 10 minutes in a warm place

Add flour and salt to an electric mixer with hook attachment

Add olive oil to the water with yeast

While mixing, add all liquid slowly

Cling film the bowl when all the flour comes away from the edges and allow to prove for 1 hour

Remove from bowl and place on tray

Stretch dough with your hands to reach all corners of the tray

Push down with your fingers

Add as much tomatoes, garlic and rosemary as you like

Leave to prove for another 45 minutes

Bake in oven at 180°C for 15 minutes

BRIOCHE

TASTE PROFILE:

This is a great quick and easy recipe that takes just over an hour, unlike traditional brioche recipes that can takes days! Full of buttery goodness, the end result is a really versatile bread that goes with so many different accompaniments.

Serves: 12

Sweet:　 ❶❷❸❹❺❻
Sour:　 ❶❷
Bitter:　 ❶
Salty:　 ❶❷❸❹
Umami:　 ❶❷❸

FOR THE BASE

500g strong flour

25g fresh yeast

75ml milk

15g salt

50g sugar

1 large egg, for the egg wash

FOR REGULAR BRIOCHE

4 egg yolks

2 large eggs

275g soft butter

FOR RICH BRIOCHE

6 egg yolks

2 large eggs

500g butter

Make a ferment of milk, sugar, yeast and leave to activate for 15-20 minutes

Sieve flour and mix in all base ingredients with the eggs and egg yolks

Add butter and mix into a smooth elastic dough

Leave to prove for 30 minutes

Knock back and rest for 40 minutes

Mould into shape and leave to prove until doubled in size

Brush with egg wash twice during proving stage

Sprinkle with crumb mix or sesame seeds

Bake at 160°C-180°C for 20-25 minutes

SOURDOUGH

TASTE PROFILE:

A simple recipe that doesn't require days of fermenting if you have the correct flour. Go to a good baker and ask for Campaillou flour – it's well worth investing in.

Sweet:	0 1 2 3 4
Sour:	0 1 2 3
Bitter:	0 1 2 3 4
Salty:	0 1 2 3 4
Umami:	0 1 2 3 4 5 6

FOR THE DOUGH

1kg Campaillou flour

20g salt

10g fresh yeast

800ml warm water

Mix all ingredients and leave to ferment for 45-60 minutes

After this time turn and dust with the flour to refresh and feed the dough

Remove from mixer and place on table for 10-15 minutes

Roll into shape

Line baking trays with baking paper

Put dough onto trays and leave for 10 minutes

Brush with water and cut to desired size

Prove until doubled in size

Brush once more with water

Place in oven at 230°C and bake for 30 minutes

AMAZU PICKLING LIQUID

200ml rice wine vinegar
150g sugar
12g salt

Bring all to the ingredients to the boil until the salt and sugar has dissolved

BEURRE NOISETTE

200g butter
Small bunch thyme

Dice the butter into small pieces

Place a saucepan on the heat and once hot add the butter, shaking the pot on the heat to make frothy

When the outside begins to colour, combine with the rest of the butter to give a consistent colour

Add your thyme to a sieve

Pour your brown butter through the sieve to infuse with thyme and allow the butter to set

BURNT LEMON JUICE AND PURÉE

12 lemons (this will give you 600ml burnt lemon juice)
350g simple stock syrup
50g sugar
15g agar
100ml water

Slice the lemons in half

Place a large frying pan on a high heat

Place the lemons, cut side down, in the pan

Char them in the pan until blackened

Remove the lemons and allow to rest

Squeeze out the juice and pass through a sieve until you get 600ml

In a saucepan bring the burnt lemon juice and stock syrup to a gentle boil

When the liquid is boiling mix in the agar and sugar and cook for 30 seconds

Pour into a container and rest in a fridge for 24 hours

To make a purée blend the juice in a blender until smooth

Combine with approximately 100ml water until it forms a mayonnaise-like consistency

CELERIAC CRUMB (OR ANY VEGETABLE CRUMB)

50g celeriac, diced

50g red rooster potatoes, diced

Oil for deep frying

Salt and pepper to season

Dice the celeriac and potatoes

Add to blender and top with water

Blitz until almost smooth then pass through a fine sieve and squeeze away any water

Rinse the mix, while still in the sieve under running water until it runs clear

Pat dry on a clean tea towel

In a large pan add the oil and bring to a medium heat

Add the vegetables carefully whisking continuously to ensure it doesn't stick together

When golden brown remove from the oil and pat the crumbs dry

Mix with some chopped truffle scrap, season then store in an airtight container

CHICKEN STOCK

2½kg chicken carcass

3 onions

3 large carrots

1 bunch celery

25g thyme

5 bay leaves

1 bulb garlic

Wash chicken bones

Place in saucepan and fill with cold water

Bring to boil

Reduce heat and simmer for 6 hours, skimming every 15 minutes

Cut vegetables into large pieces and add to stock

Cook for 3 hours skimming every 15 minutes

Pass through sieve and drain stock

COURT BOUILLON

1 large carrot, thinly sliced

1 large onion, thinly sliced

1 celery stalk, thinly sliced

2 cloves garlic, thinly sliced

1 bouquet garni

1 tsp fennel seeds

1 tsp white peppercorns

1 star anise

3 tbsp coarse sea salt

500ml dry white wine

2 tsp white vinegar

4 litres water

Thinly slice the vegetables

In a large stockpot combine the vegetables, herbs, spices, salt and water

Bring to the boil then cook over a high heat for 20 minutes

Once boiled reduce the heat to a simmer, add the wine and vinegar and simmer for another 5 minutes

Strain the court bouillon through muslin

Court bouillon may be refrigerated for up to 2 days but should not be frozen as it can become bitter

CURRY OIL

500g vegetable oil
1 Granny Smith apple, thinly sliced
4 shallots, thinly sliced
1 lemongrass, thinly sliced
30g masala curry powder
2 kaffir lime leaves
Salt and pepper to season

Heat half of the oil
Thinly slice the apple, shallots and lemongrass
Gently fry in the oil until see-through
When cooked add the curry powder and lightly caramelise
Add the remaining oil and lime leaves
Cook gently for 5 minutes, do not boil
Remove from the heat and sit for 30 minutes
Pour through a coffee filter and season to taste

DARK CHICKEN STOCK

2½kg chicken wings
50ml vegetable oil
5 litres chicken stock
1 litre red wine
1 bulb garlic
200g mushrooms
6 shallots
5 sprigs of thyme
2 bay leaves

Rinse the chicken wings in cold water and place on a roasting try with the oil and cook in a hot oven until golden brown
Roast the shallots, garlic and mushroom until golden
Deglaze with red wine
Add herbs
Add chicken wings
Top up with stock
Simmer skimming regularly
Remove from the heat and pass through muslin
Return the stock to a saucepan and reduce by half

DILL OIL

2 bunches dill
150ml vegetable oil
Salt and pepper to season

Pick the dill and blanche in salted water for 7 seconds then refresh in iced water
Lay half out on a tray and leave to dry slightly
Once dry weighout 100g of dill
Add to blender and blend with 150ml veg oil for 1 minute
Place the blending jug in the fridge for 10 minutes
Repeat the process twice
Once blended cool instantly to preserve the colour
Season to taste

FISH STOCK

50ml olive oil

1 leek

1 onion

2 stalks celery

2 cloves garlic

2kg white fish bones

4 coriander seeds

250ml white wine

3 sprigs of parsley

2 sprigs thyme

1 lemon

2½ litres water

Prepare the onion, celery, garlic and lemon by chopping them into chunks, and slice the leeks

Clean and roughly chop the fish bones and place in water until needed

Place the vegetables in a saucepan with preheated oil and sweat until soft

Add the fish bones and coriander seeds and sweat again

Add the wine and reduce until almost evaporated

Add the water, herbs and lemon, and bring to the boil skimming the stock

Reduce the heat and allow to simmer for 20 minutes

Remove from the heat and allow the stock to settle for about 15 minutes

Carefully tilt the stockpot to one side and pass the stock through a strainer lined with muslin being careful not to disturb the flesh and bones at the base of the stock

NAGE (VEGETABLE STOCK)

2 carrots

1 onions

2 sticks celery

½ celeriac

1 large leek

1 tsp coriander seeds

1 star anise

2 juniper berries

2 cardamom seeds

3 tsp fennel seeds

3 black peppercorns

3 red peppercorns

100ml chardonnay

½ bunch chives

½ bunch chervil

½ bunch tarragon

1 lemons, zest

Chop the vegetables and wash them under cold water

Place in a large saucepan and cover with water

Bring to the boil and simmer for 20 minutes

While vegetables are simmering, crush all spices then add to the saucepan

Add the herbs, wine and lemon zest and bring back to the boil

Remove from the heat and allow cooling for a short while

Cover with cling film and leave to stand for 24 hours

Once the stock is cool, pass through muslin and place in refrigerator

NAPPAGE

500ml water
500g sugar
20g pectin

Add water and sugar to a pot and bring to the boil
Whisk in the pectin and allow to boil for 30 seconds
Pass through a sieve and leave to cool
This can be kept for up to one month in the fridge

PONZU

250ml rice wine vinegar
125ml litres soy sauce
35ml lemon juice

Ponzu is a tart dipping sauce
Combine all the ingredients

SIMPLE STOCK SYRUP

100g sugar
130ml water

Add the sugar and water to a saucepan and bring to a boil until the sugar dissolves but doesn't colour

Remove from the heat and allow to cool

VEAL STOCK

5kg veal bones
300g carrots, peeled and chopped
400g leeks, peeled and chopped
200g onions, peeled and chopped
1 head garlic, split
1 small handful parsley stalks
2 bay leaves
½ bunch thyme
8 tomatoes

Prepare the vegetables by peeling and cutting into 2 inch chunks

Rinse the bones in cold water and drain well

Place the bones in a roasting tray with half the vegetables and half the oil and roast on a high heat until golden brown

Roast the remaining vegetables with the remaining oil in a separate tray until golden brown

Place the bones and vegetables in a stockpot, add herbs and cover with water

Bring to a boil and skim, reduce the heat to a simmer and add the tomato puree

Simmer gently for 6-8 hours, skimming at least every hour

Reduce the stock to around 4 litres

Strain through muslin